LUKE'S NOTEBOOK

Meditations on the Gospel

by

Frank (Rev. Francis) Colborn

ISBN 978-0-557-15306-0

FOREWORD

Luke 1:1-4

Dear reader, beloved by God, loving God:

Many people have tried to give us an orderly account of what the first witnesses of the word have handed down to us.

I, too, have decided to try my hand at it, after doing some research of my own…

… in order to reaffirm what you know of your faith.

This is a meditation, or rather, a series of meditations, on the Gospel of Luke. Even more precisely, it is an invitation to meditation on the Gospel. It is not a novel. It is not a work of history. What a reader will find here is a series of imaginary scenes, taken from different parts of Luke's Gospel. The stories feature minor characters or people not even mentioned in the original Gospel of Luke, but who must have been present when Jesus was speaking and acting. They are people a little bit like ourselves: not famous, not heroes, but ordinary people who are challenged by what they see and hear.

On the margin of each page is a sidebar with a verse or a few verses from the real Gospel according to St. Luke, in my own rather free translation from the original.

At the conclusion of each scene are some questions for personal reflection, which may lead to deeper meditation on the meaning of the real Gospel for the reader. These are suggested; your own questions may offer better reflection starters. In the end, you may have some things to say to the Lord.

I am neither trying to reconstruct the "real Jesus of history," nor pretending that I know exactly how Jesus of Nazareth would have acted if he had lived in modern times. This is a work of imagination, and readers may enjoy using their own imaginations to improve on my answers to questions like these. What's the equivalent, in a modern urban society, of shepherds of ancient times? Of tax collectors and business people in Roman Palestine? How would someone a bit like Jesus impress people more or less like us, in a world somewhat like our own? What would they make of him? What would they say about him?

What would you think of him? Of course, this leads toward the question: *what you think of the real Jesus of Nazareth, who still lives and still speaks to us?*

INTRODUCTION
Luke 1:1-4

What would Jesus do…if Jesus were born in our time?

> **Luke 1:1-4**
>
> **Dear reader, beloved by God, loving God:**
>
> **Many people have tried to give us an orderly account of what the first witnesses of the word have handed down to us.**
>
> **I, too, have decided to try my hand at it, after doing some research of my own…**
>
> **… in order to reaffirm what you know of your faith.**

Many books, movies and plays have suggested different answers to that question. I, too, have tried to imagine what it would be like, if Jesus were born now instead of two thousand years ago.

Of course, if Jesus had not been born in Roman-occupied Palestine, two thousand years ago, the world today would be different than it is. Yet there might still have been a Jewish revolt against Rome, and Roman armies might have crushed it and destroyed Jerusalem and the Temple. In the Jewish communities scattered throughout the Empire, various quasi-Jewish sects might have arisen, and one of them might in time have taken over the Empire. When the Roman Empire fell, from its ashes would arise, not Western Christendom, but perhaps Western Gnostic Civilization. There could be a Universal Gnostic Church, still possessed of the Hebrew Scriptures (our Old Testament), a Renaissance, a Reformation, and an Age of Enlightenment…and then a "modern world". I imagine that world as somewhat like our own, but harsher, colder, meaner – somewhat like the world of Jesus of Nazareth.

Into this world, in my imagination, 1900 years after the fall of Jerusalem, is born a child named Jesús. At about the age of thirty, he enters the public arena, attracts followers, makes enemies, and is executed. His followers affirm that he has risen and lives.

Decades later, another young man, named Luke, begins to gather information about him, with a view toward writing a book. Of a later generation, he is also of a different social and economic class than Jesús (the original Luke was supposed to have been a physician). He is also of a different ethnic group – he has to keep reminding himself that his hero's name is pronounced like "hay-SOOS". As this "Luke" gathers material, he keeps it in a notebook, which gradually becomes a collection of journal entries, newspaper clippings, tape recordings and transcriptions. The pages that follow are the bits and pieces that "Luke" hopes to use for his book.

PRELUDE: SONGS OF FREEDOM (MARY'S SONG)
Luke 1:5-2:40
(Journal entry)

I'm trying to write a book. All I've got are bits and pieces. I keep thinking I'll give it up, but then I keep running into people who won't let me quit. Like my old friend, the one I will always think of as the Freedom Singer.

I first heard her sing at a backyard barbecue in East L.A. She was quite young then, her black hair worn waist length, her eyes bright, her voice high and pure – and loud.

> *"The folks with power, they've got guns,*
> *We folks without, we've got our God,*
> *And God will give us victory!"*

Luke 1: 51-53

Mary's words: "His strong arm has done powerful things: he has put down the high and mighty, and has raised up the poor and humble. In his mercy, He has taken care of his people."

"What if a neighbor called the Security Force?" I dared to ask her when she paused for a break. I learned then that "snapping eyes" is not a physically impossible figure of speech. She snapped at me, visually and verbally.

"What do I care? They going to arrest us all?"

Since all of us were only a dozen people hanging around hungrily sniffing the carne asada on the barbecue, I thought, yes, they just might do that. But she picked up her guitar and raised her voice again:

> *"The proud and rich, God puts them down,*
> *The poor and low, God lifts them up,*
> *There isn't any fear in me!*

I was silenced by a mix of admiration and fear and shame and a desire to know where she got the spirit that filled her.

I hadn't seen her for years, but today she came into the coffee shop where I was sitting and recognized me immediately and sat down to talk. I reminded her of that backyard scene from years past. She laughed and said, "We were a feisty bunch in those days, weren't we? Some of us more than others."

I reminded her that I had been a newcomer in those days, trying to find out what this talk of Jesús was about, and had felt a bit out of place among her friends, even though they had invited me to the barbecue. Then I showed her the notebook in which I was collecting material for my book on Jesús. She said, "If you're doing that kind of research, I have something for you in my garage: a picture of one of our songwriters. Come on over."

So I went, and she led me into an old garage, and unveiled an ancient eight-millimeter home movie projector. I didn't think such things still existed. It took her some time to get the picture focused. When she did, I was surprised. I guess I expected to see an aging Chicano hippie. Instead the image on the garage wall looked like a very respectable accountant or bank clerk, seated with erect posture, dressed in suit and tie. And he was not aged, though a bit old to be the proud papa of the baby he was holding in his arms. When my friend got the sound working, scratchy as it was, we could hear him singing, softly,

"Little boy, you are going to light God's way;
Little boy, you'll show us the dawn of day…"

A voice from someone off-screen said, "Deacon Zachary, tell us what happened."

A woman, herself no longer young, came up behind him and kissed him on the top of the head, and told him, "Go ahead, Zacarías. I can stand to hear it again. I've missed the sound of your voice."

The man laughed. "That's the last thing I ever expected to hear from you. You know," he said, looking toward the person holding the camera, "It might have been different if Isabel hadn't got tired of listening to me talk and made me go to the cathedral by myself…I know you all call her Elizabeth, but I call her Isabel, because she likes it, but she always complains I talk too much…"

"Just tell us the story, Uncle Zack," another off-screen voice broke in.

"All right. You know we deacons from outside the city are invited to the cathedral every so often to lead Sunday Evensong. Well, about nine months ago, it was my turn, and I wanted Isabel to go with me, but she wanted some time to herself, some peace and quiet, I guess, so I drove down alone. Since they finished the freeway, it's only about twenty minutes from here in Tujunga to the Cathedral and I like the drive. So anyway I got there in plenty of time that evening, and parked near the sacristy, and went up the steps, and in the door, and there was a stranger standing near the table where the incense is prepared. Now that's my job – I mean, it's the deacon's job to prepare the incense for the service. And I didn't know who this guy was. Maybe he'd broken into the sacristy to steal something. So I go right up to him, and I say, 'Who are you?'

Luke 1:76-77

Zachary's song: "You, child, shall be a prophet of the Most High God… You will tell of salvation for God's people, and prepare the way of the Lord, to bring light to those who sit in darkness, and guide us to peace."

Luke 1:5-25

There was a priest named Zachariah, whose wife was Elizabeth… When his turn came, he went to the Temple. A messenger from God spoke to him, standing by the altar of incense.

The messenger said: "You wife is going to bear a child… He will be great, and will convert the hearts of many…"

Zachariah said, "How can I believe this?"

He said, "You will be mute, until the child is born!" Zachariah had to make signs to the people gathered for the service.

"And he says to me, 'My name's Gabriel.' And he sticks out his hand, but I'm not going to shake hands with him till I know what he's doing there. And I want to ask him, but I also want to be polite and ask him, 'How do you do?' But I'm nervous, and it comes out, 'What do you do?'

"And he says, 'I'm in communications. And I have a message for you. Your wife Isabel is going to have a baby. That's great news, isn't it? You can have a great party on his naming day - and by the way, name him Juan. Or John, if you prefer. He's going to be a great preacher, filled with God's spirit, and God will be with him. And he'll bring many people to God.' That's what he said. Well, he said it better than I'm saying it, more formal, more like poetry."

Zachary shifted a little in his chair, looking uncomfortable. "You wouldn't expect me to believe him, would you? In fact, I got pretty mad, and started going on about how my family life was none of his business, and who did he think he was, anyhow, and he got that look Isabel sometimes gets when I go on too long, and finally he says to me, 'For God's sake, Zachary, shut up!' And then he looks kind of sorry he said it, 'cause I really shut up, I mean, my lips kept moving, but I couldn't get a word out. I shut my eyes and pretended for a second that none of this was happening, and when I opened them, the stranger was gone. And I haven't said a word since, until today. It was really embarrassing to get the people who'd come to Evensong to understand that I couldn't lead the service. But it's worth it to have our little boy, isn't it?"

At this the baby began to fuss a bit in his father's arms. Then a younger woman came into the picture and said, "I'll hold him a while, Uncle Zachary," and took the child up and left the picture.

"That's her," my friend said. "That's Maria. *The* Maria."

"You're kidding," I said. "How do you know that?"

"I met her once," she said.

"When? Where?"

She turned off the projector, looked at me, and began to reminisce.

"When I was just a little girl, my parents took me on a trip up to the Bay area, where she was living at the time. We drove right up to the front of her little bungalow. There she was on the front porch. To a little girl like me she looked like a real old lady, all gray hair and wrinkles. But when she smiled, it was like she was everybody's *madre* – or *abuelita*, anyway. You know, grandmother?"

"I know what *abuelita* means."

"Of course you do. Well, she took me in her arms and held me on her lap while she and my parents talked. Most of it was over my head, and when she saw I was getting drowsy, she began to sing to me, very softly,

> '*Be glad, mi'jita, God's own child,*
> *God smiles on you…*'

"And that's how I first heard Maria's Song."

"Did you learn anything else?"

"Oh, she told me a story of when she was young, not a lot older than me, she said, and she was washing dishes in her parents' kitchen, and this stranger walked in the door. She said the stranger looked a little like Julio Iglesias, but maybe eight feet tall. You know who Julio Iglesias was?"

"Some singer who used to be famous?"

"Yeah, and handsome. She was so scared she dropped a plate and yelled for her mom, but her mom was in the back yard and didn't hear her. And the stranger said she should not be afraid because God had a special love for her. She was trying to dry her hands on her blouse and not to show how nervous she was. The stranger had a voice like the surf when it's up and breaking on the rocks. He told her she was going to have a baby and name him Jesús. Well, she had a sort of understanding with a man named José, but her parents thought she was too young to get married, and anyway he didn't have enough money – he was just a garage mechanic in a small town -- and there was no way she was going to go with him without being married. But the stranger said not to worry, God would take care of everything, God's Spirit would fill her, and her baby would be God's own son, and would save his people."

"She could understand that?"

"Anybody could understand the people needed saving. Things were really bad back then for just about everyone."

"But she went along with this program?"

Luke 1:47-48

Mary's words: "My whole being rejoices in God, whose face gazes on this lowly maidservant."

Luke 1:26-38

The angel Gabriel was sent from God to a virgin named Mary, who was engaged to a man named Joseph….

"Don't be afraid… You will have a child who will be savior of his people…It will be by the power of the Holy Spirit…"

Mary said, "I am the Lord's servant. Let it be as you say."

"I asked her about that. She said, 'What's a girl going to say to an eight-foot tall version of Julio Iglesias with a voice like the ocean?' But she laughed and I knew she was teasing. Then she said, 'Really, there's one thing I always knew, my parents taught me, and I never doubted it for a second -- that God loved me and what God wanted for me had to be good. So I said that if this was God's plan, I was at God's service – *a sus órdenes*.' That's how Maria told me the story."

"Wait a minute," I said. "What about that lullaby? That's not what you were singing when I first met you. That was all power and strength and courage…"

"I was just a little girl on her lap. You don't think she was going to belt out a freedom song in my ear, do you? Besides, there are lots of versions of Maria's Song. Some you hear in prayer meetings, others at rallies and marches, others in people's backyards *¿verdad*? Wherever people gather with faith and hope."

"Yeah, I've heard the songs, but I didn't always think of them as Maria's Song. A lot of them seemed like verses from Scripture."

"So? Don't you think Maria knew how to quote the Book? And anyway, she probably sang it herself in different ways at different times. What she sang to me, she said, was one of the things she and Isabel sang together when Maria was visiting her, just before Isabel's baby was born."

[Questions for reflection:
When you think of Mary the mother of Jesus, do you imagine her as a young girl, a mature matron, an elderly lady, or as a glorious Queen? If you could spend some time with her, what would you ask her about? We sometimes sing the canticle of Mary as a hymn in church. Can you imagine it as a lullaby, or a folk song, or a Gospel hymn, or a marching song? What do you make of its message?]

(ZACHARY'S SONG)

"So you figure it's Maria in the picture," I said to my friend, not exactly meaning to challenge her.

"Of course it is. Want to see some more?"

Without waiting for an answer, she flipped the switch, and we could see Zachary again. The person with the camera had stepped back and now we could see, behind Zachary, people holding hand-lettered signs. One said, "JOHN" and the other "JUAN". Zachary had picked up a guitar and began to sing again.

"Our God has come to set us free,
Free from our deadly enemy;
He gives us light that we may see—
See justice and live peacefully."

At that the projector clattered and wheezed to a stop.

"What do you expect?" my friend asked. "It's a wonder it's worked this long."

[Questions for reflection:
Zachary says God has come to set us free. From what do God's people need to be set free nowadays? From what do you need to be set free?]

Luke 2:1-20
A decree came from the emperor Augustus Caesar, that everyone should register. Joseph went from Nazareth to Bethlehem (which in Hebrew means "House of Bread"), to register. While they were there, her child was born – and laid in a manger, for there was no room for them in a regular hostelry.

"I've got something else for you," my friend said.

"Another song?"

"Yes, as a matter of fact. While Maria was talking to me she told me a story of the time when Jesús was born. She and José were officially married by then, and she went down south with him to Anaheim, where his relatives lived – some business about straightening out his papers, some government order that some bureaucrat had thought up. But when they got there, the cousins he was supposed to stay with didn't have any room, and José still didn't have any money, so the cousins let them stay overnight in a garage behind the bakery they owned. It was called "La Casa de Pan;" Maria remembered that name. That was where her baby was born. And she gave me another story, and another song, and I wrote it down, in my own words, later on. Here—you can put it in that notebook you're carrying around."

(SONG OF THE ARMIES OF THE LORD)

[insert into notebook]

THE NIGHT WATCHMEN'S STORY

THERE WERE WATCHMEN IN THE NEIGHBORHOOD, KEEPING WATCH BY NIGHT OVER A PARKING LOT FULL OF CARS, FROM A SHED IN THE MIDDLE OF THE LOT. THE SHED HAD A HEATER AND A SMALL TV, BUT NEITHER WORKED. LOUIE WAS ON UNTIL MIDNIGHT, WHEN HE WAS RELIEVED BY LUIS. ALMOST EVERY NIGHT THEY HAD THE SAME CONVERSATION.

"HOW YOU DOIN', LOUIE?"

"SAME AS ALWAYS. COLD. SINCE THEY BUSTED THE UNION, THEY DON'T HAVE TO FIX NO HEATER FOR NO BLACK MAN. NOR FOR NO MEXICAN, NEITHER."

"I'M NOT MEXICAN," LUIS WOULD RESPOND. "SO WHAT'S ON TV?"

"SAME AS ALWAYS," LOUIE WOULD SAY. "YOU KNOW THAT SCREEN'S BEEN DEAD FOR YEARS."

BUT THIS NIGHT, JUST AS HE SAID IT, THE SCREEN LIT UP, VERY, VERY BRIGHT, AND AN ANNOUNCER APPEARED. BOTH LUIS AND LOUIE GULPED AND STARED.

"THERE'S BREAKING NEWS, BUT NO CAUSE FOR PANIC," SAID THE NEWSCASTER. "THIS JUST IN: TODAY A CHILD, A LEADER CONSECRATED BY GOD TO SAVE GOD'S PEOPLE, HAS BEEN BORN... FOR YOU."

"NOT LIKELY FOR ME," SAID LOUIE. "NOT FOR NO BLACK MAN. AND NOT FOR NO MEXICAN, NEITHER."

"I'M NOT MEXICAN," LUIS PROTESTED.

THE ANNOUNCER'S VOICE GREW MORE STERN. "THE SIGN THAT THIS CHILD IS FOR YOU IS THIS: YOU WILL FIND HIM IN A GARAGE IN THE BARRIO NEAREST TO YOU."

AND SUDDENLY THERE WAS WITH THE ANNOUNCER A HUGE ARMY, AS THE CAMERA PANNED TO A WIDER VIEW: THOUSANDS MARCHING, CARRYING NO WEAPONS, BUT APPEARING UNSTOPPABL, INVINCIBLE. THEY WERE SINGING, AND LOUIE AND LUIS WERE CARRIED ALONG BY THEIR SONG:

> *"GLORY, GLORY, HALLELUJAH!*
> *¡GLORIA, GLORIA, ALLELUIA!*
> *GOD GIVES HIS PEOPLE PEACE!*

And there were shepherds in the area, watching over their flocks at night. An angel, a messenger from God, appeared and told them, "Do not be afraid; I bring you great good news; today a savior is born for you... And this will be the sign for you: you will find the child in a manger."

And suddenly there appeared with the heavenly messenger a whole army from heaven, singing, "Glory to God! Peace to God's people!"

The shepherds said to one another, "Let us go see what has happened!" And they found Mary and Joseph and the child...

And Mary kept all this like a treasure in her heart.

THE SCREEN WENT BLANK.

LUIS HELD UP THE ELECTRIC CORD THAT DANGLED FROM THE TV SET. "IT AIN'T JUST BROKE," HE POINTED OUT. "IT AIN'T EVEN PLUGGED IN."

LOUIE SAID, "COME ON, WE GOT TO CHECK THIS OUT. CARS CAN WATCH THEMSELVES FOR A WHILE."

THEY DROVE AROUND IN LUIS'S OLD PICKUP UNTIL THEY SAW A GARAGE WITH A LIGHT ON INSIDE. THEY WENT IN AND FOUND THE CHILD AND MARIA AND JOSÉ. OF COURSE THEY TOLD THE PARENTS WHAT THEY'D SEEN AND HEARD. AND OF COURSE MARIA REMEMBERED IT, AND TOLD IT TO ME, AND I HAVE WRITTEN IT DOWN, IN MY OWN STYLE.

[Questions:
Under what circumstances do you imagine Jesus being born in our world today?
If you could visit Mary and Joseph just after Jesus' birth, what would you say to them?]

"That's a great story," I said when I had read it.

"But…?"

"But what?"

"But you think I made it up."

"No, not that. But this is a lot to take in. I don't know what to make of it all."

"So," she sniffed, "You'll just have to make of it what you can, when you come to write your book. But I'll tell you something you might make of it: God's Spirit works in women at least as much as in men."

"Belabor the obvious," I muttered.

She ignored me and continued, "And God's Spirit blesses not the high and mighty but ordinary people."

"You mean poor folks," I said.

"Practically every one of us was poor in those days."

"But we're not all poor now," I pointed out. "Some of us are pretty well off, and others are hoping to be…"

"Maybe that's why you need to write that book," she told me. "Maybe we need to be reminded of where we came from."

We were both silent for a minute, as she began to rewind, by hand, the film on the projector. Then she suggested, "Why don't you go down to the desert to do some research? That's where the message from God came to Zachary's son John."

"Been there, done that," I told her with some satisfaction. "I went there quite early in my research. Want to see what I've got in my notebook about it?"

So we sat and leafed through the notebook together.

THE SHERIFF'S STORY

Luke 3:1-22

Luke 3:1-22

In the fifteenth year of the reign of Tiberias Caesar, when Pontius Pilate governed Judea, and Herod Galilee, and his brother Philip Iturea…when a Annas and Caiaphas were the chief priests -- the word of God came to John, son of Zacharias, in the desert.
And he came to the region of the Jordan River, and proclaimed a baptism of conversion, so that sins could be forgiven….

[photocopy of editorial from Desert and Mountain Herald]

SHERIFF THROCK, ACT NOW!

This is the fifteenth year of the Harriman Administration. The Southern California Military District is under the watchful eye of General Pilato. Governor Herrold is taking good care of the state as a whole, as his brother Philip is doing for Nevada. As for religious leaders, we are blessed with (among others) Archbishop Hannon and Bishop Califas, as he calls himself.

Why, then, do we need some outside agitator to come into our beautiful valleys and canyons and demand a total change in the way we do things? In case you haven't heard, a certain religious fanatic named John (or is it Juan?) has been polluting our desert air with calls for an end to business as usual, while his bearded, scruffy followers pollute the streams in the canyon where they gather.

With the other respectable citizens of our desert communities, we wonder why the authorities have let this dropout from a monastery rant on for so long. We call on Sheriff Throck to act now to put an end to this dangerous nonsense. If he does not, higher authorities may have to intervene.

--- --- --- --- --- --- ---

[partial transcript of an interview with ex-Sheriff Throck]

Found my address in the phone book, huh? Not too many Throcks in this part of the world. But how'd you learn my name? An old editorial from the news archives, you say? Thought they'd purged all that stuff. Guess they missed one piece.

Bet you didn't expect a man retired from a long career as sheriff to be living in a dumpy trailer in North Palm Springs, did you? Well, I didn't have a long career. Sure, I'll tell you about it.

I sure do remember that editorial. That's what got me in trouble. I'd heard about this John fella, or Juan, as some people called him, and about the crowds that went to hear him preach, but I'd figured my deputies had everything under control. I took that editorial as a signal from higher up that I'd better get personally involved. So I went out to the canyon to see for myself.

It's a pretty place– it's just south of town, you know? – stream running through it, trees along the edge of the stream, plenty of space for people to gather round and hear John talk.

And he was some talker, I'll tell you. Said God had given him a message. Said he was descended from some of the Native Americans who used to live around these springs. Said some others of his ancestors had come up from Mexico with the settlers who founded Los Angeles. Told about how they had hiked up through the desert and stopped at these springs before climbing over the pass toward the West. Claimed he had a message from God: it was time to make a new beginning, to be washed clean in these waters again and go back over that pass to reconstruct the cities. Said he wasn't going to make it happen – that was for someone else to do – but he was the messenger, announcing a new day to come. Well, he had me going along with him for a bit. Not that I was going to go into that stream and wash. I'm not a religious man. But it seemed like a nice idea that we all could make a fresh start. But I'm not a very courageous man, either.

And the crowd that had turned out to hear him wasn't all long-haired hippies. There were even clergy types there. John laid into them good. Called 'em snakes. Told 'em to start acting like godly men or they'd get cut off at the knees – something like that.

And there were guys in suits from the big city, too. John got after them, too. Reminded them that some of them had more suits than they could ever wear. "Some of you got more cars than you need. Some of you even got more houses than you need! And there are people all around you with nothing! Give some of that stuff away! You don't need that consumer confidence we're always hearing about – you need giver confidence!" That kind of thing.

Some government bureaucrat asked him for guidance on how to live. He just laughed and said, "It's not that complicated. Just do your job and quit taking bribes." The guy who asked didn't laugh, though. I mean, what's the point of having a position of power if you don't use it to take care of yourself and your family?

One of my deputies yells, "And what do you expect us to do?" And John says, "Don't lean on people for money. Cut out the dirty busts and the false charges. Learn to live on your salaries and do without the *mordida*." Well, I could hear my guys snickering at that bit of dreaming.

In the middle of all this, there's a lull. And this other young man comes walking down to the side of the stream. Learned later it was Jesús – but he wasn't famous then. He's dressed in jeans and

---

He said to the crowds: "You race of vipers! Don't be claiming to be children of Abraham…The axe is already poised to strike the trees at the roots!"

They said to him, "What should we do?" He said, "Those who have two coats should give one to someone who has none…"

To the tax collectors who came he said, "Don't take more than the established rate."

To the soldiers he said, "No violence, no lies: be content with your pay."

Luke 3:21-22

When everyone was baptized, and Jesus was baptized, the sky was opened and the Holy Spirit came down upon, in a visible way... like a dove. And a voice came from the sky, that said, "You are my beloved son; I am happy with you."

[See the Gospel of John's account, which is a little different.]

casual shirt, like most of the people there. He's kind of medium height, maybe a little taller. From where I'm standing, at the back of the crowd, I don't see anything special about him. But all of a sudden everybody's watching him. He says something to John – I couldn't hear it – and John shakes his head, and they talk a little more, and then the two of them wade into the stream and John is scooping up water with his hands and pouring it over him.

And then there's a moment of absolute silence. And the sky gets very bright for an instant, I mean, it was already bright, but for a second I was just blinded by the brightness. And I thought I heard thunder – but it was a clear day and there weren't any clouds. Maybe it was something else – I'm just telling you what I thought at the time. What I mean is, there was something really strange there. For a minute it was completely clear and quiet. I mean, we're used to quiet in the desert, but here were all these people around, and it was as silent as if we were in church – I mean the old-fashioned kind of church. What I thought to myself was, the Spirit of God is here, coming down into this canyon. And I'm not a religious man.

What did I do? I did what I had to do. I picked up my bullhorn and said, "This is an unlawful assembly! Break it up or you'll be arrested." And my deputies started raising their sticks, but they didn't have to use them. Everybody just walked away, nice as anything. John-Juan and Jesús, too, just went off somewhere. Course they were all back there the next day. I knew what would happen, but I'd done my job.

And then I went home and wrote my letter of resignation. Never had another job in law enforcement.

Why'd I quit? Didn't I make myself clear? I'm not religious, and I'm not courageous, and I knew what was going to happen. They weren't going to let John go on like that, and when he went after the Governor for his personal life, they went after John and got him. I wasn't going to be a follower of John, and I sure wasn't going to follow Jesús, but I wasn't going to arrest either of them. I knew God had come into that canyon that day. And if I didn't want to stand up to the high mucky-mucks who wanted John's head, I sure wasn't going to fight with God.

So here I am, in this grungy trailer park, and better off for it.

*[Questions:
If you were in the crowd listening to a contemporary John the Baptist, what would you ask him? What would he respond? How would you react?]*

WHERE DID HE COME FROM?

Luke 3: 23-38

[notes on genealogical research]

After hearing from the sheriff what John had said about his ancestors, I got wondering about Jesús' family tree.

His appeal cut across all racial and ethnic lines. Mexican Americans considered him a member of *la raza,* and he was evidently proud of his Latino heritage, and, by all accounts, could be eloquent in either English or Spanish. But Filipinos identified with him too. And many African Americans, watching and listening to him, were sure he was Black.

In the decades since his death, of course, his following has become international.

As far as I can determine, Jesús shared the lineage of John/Juan. That is, his ancestry could be traced back to the first *pobladores de Los Angeles,* who had come up from Mexico.

Now those early settlers were a very mixed group, racially. Their ancestors included Spanish conquistadors and indigenous Mexicans (of royal blood, perhaps, somewhere in the past?) and African captives brought to the New World as slaves. Some of them may have had Asian genes as well, brought to western Mexico by the Manila galleons.

Beyond that, the common heritage goes back, if the theories about mitochondrial DNA are correct, to that ancient "Eve" who lived in East Africa many millennia ago.

So perhaps everyone is right to claim a part of him.

[Does Jesus' ancestry make a difference?]

Luke 3:23-38

Jesus was then approaching the age of thirty. He was thought to be the son of Joseph, who was the son of Heli, who was the son of Mathat ... ... the son of David ... ... the son of Abraham ... ... the son of Adam, who came from God.

IN THE WILDERNESS

Luke 4:1-13

[old journal entry, recently rewritten]

Luke 4:1-13

Jesus, filled with holy spirit, was led by the spirit into deserted areas, for forty days, experiencing testing by the devil.
He did not eat anything during these days, and by the end of the time he was hungry.

I had heard that after the encounter with John, Jesús disappeared for a while. He was known to spend a lot of time alone, thinking and praying about what he would do next. There were trails through the desert and mountains that led toward the coast, back toward Jesús' home town. I thought I might get in touch with his spirit by hiking along those trails myself, alone. It took me weeks. I didn't have much to eat. I got pretty tired and hungry. On the other hand, I had a lot of time to get in touch with myself and to read the Scriptures, and to think about how Jesús directed his life, and about what I should do. Apparently he got a lot of free advice about what he should do, some of it well-meaning, some of it less so. Some people talked about how he gradually came to a sense of his mission. Those who had known him personally claimed that he always seemed sure of who he was and what he was about. I thought about these matters a lot as I hiked through the San Gabriel Mountains, up high where the pines grow, heading west.

One evening I got tired early and stopped to sit and rest. I sat down on a fallen log and got out the Book and began reading Deuteronomy. I had a hard time concentrating and kept dozing off.

A stranger came walking along the trail and caught me napping. I woke up, or thought I did, and sat upright. The stranger was standing over me, looking at the Book in my lap.

"Looks like you've got one of them new modern translations," he said. "Can't say they ever did much for me."

"Well, it helps me," I said, "to think about the direction of my life."

"The direction of your life? What's the problem? You're young. You're smart. You're idealistic. Might say you're one of God's blessed children. You want to do good, don't you?"

"Of course."

The devil said to him, "If you are the son of God, tell this stone to turn into bread."

"Well, let me give you some advice. If you want to do good, you've got to do well. Get yourself a career. Make some money. Get established. Then you'll be in a position to help other people."

My eyes fell on the Book in my lap. A sentence struck me. "It says here, 'Bread isn't the source of life – the words of God are what give life.'"

"You're pretty quick with a Scripture quote," said the stranger. "But I've heard it said that even the devil can quote Scripture. Come on, take a little walk with me."

He took my arm and pulled me to my feet and walked with me, just a short way, to where the mountainside fell away and we were looking out at the San Gabriel Valley. Up where we were, the sun had not yet set; but down below, it was dusk, and the lights were coming on. We could see the whole valley and all the way to downtown Los Angeles. It was breathtaking.

"I shouldn't have pretended to be your financial advisor," said the stranger. "I like politics better, and I'm really good at that. Now, you look down at all those lights.

"That's a lot of people living down there. They need leadership. They need someone with your good will and your brains to take charge. Believe me, I know how you can get power. I can show you the ropes. You'll climb fast. Today, Cucamonga; tomorrow, the world!" He laughed. "But if I'm going to be your political consultant, you're going to have to listen to me. You're going to have to take my advice. Can you promise me that?"

I held up the Book, which was still in my hand. "It says, 'Don't give your allegiance to anyone but God.'"

"I'll be darned," said the stranger. "I'll be doggoned. You're turning me down. Well, you're not the first."

He sighed and gazed off toward the west. "Maybe you're too religious for the political game. That's okay. Religion can be even better than politics, for my purposes." He pointed toward the towers of downtown Los Angeles. "The biggest buildings you see are banks," he said. "Next are the government buildings. You can hardly see the Cathedral from here. But there's lots of room for me – for us, I mean – to work there, too". He pointed down the range of mountains toward a row of antennas silhouetted against the setting sun. "Those are the radio and TV transmitters on Mount Wilson. Right now they're beaming out some very popular shows that feature big-time evangelists. Some of those guys rake in a lot of money. A few of them become advisors to mayors and governors and presidents. You could go that way. Just make a big show of yourself – do a couple of miracles on nationwide TV. Of course, it takes some nerve to pull that

19

Jesus: "It also says, "You shall not test the Lord your God.""

The devil left him – till a later time.

[In Mark's Gospel, "Angels came and comforted him."]

kind of thing off. But you trust in God, don't you? Doesn't your Book tell you that he'll take care of you, whatever you do?"

"Not exactly. It says God will take care of us if we are doing God's will. 'Trust God, but don't lay demands on him,' or words to that effect. And if you don't mind, I don't want to pursue this conversation. Frankly, I'm exhausted."

"So you're telling me to go to hell? You don't need to say it. I can take a hint. *Hasta la vista,* pal."

"I don't want to be your pal," I started to say, but he strode off and disappeared. I shivered. Was his "*Hasta la vista*" just words, or a warning?

I stumbled back to where I'd been sitting, lay down on the ground, and fell asleep again. Or thought I did. I had dreams of pleasant voices telling me everything was all right, I was loved, I was cared for, I was safe.

When I woke again in the morning, I wasn't sure what I had dreamed and what I had been awake for. But I knew what direction to take. I headed toward Jesús' home town.

[Were the temptations of Jesus one-time events, or were they repeated at other times in his life? Were they his alone, or are his followers tempted in similar ways? What temptations have been significant at important moments in your life? Have the words of Scripture ever occurred to you in those moments?]

HOME TOWN BOY

Luke 4:14-30

[partial transcription of interview]

Luke 4: 14-30

He came to Nazareth, where he had been brought up, and went to the synagogue on the Sabbath.

Yes, I knew Jesús. When I was a kid, he was one of the older boys. He was always nice to me.

Yes, I knew his family. His mother Maria was a nice lady. I didn't know his father very well. If José was his father. There were stories around town about that. Anyway he died before I grew up. After that, Jesús took care of his mother, until he went away; and then she would do some baby-sitting and housecleaning to help make ends meet. She still found time to do a lot of volunteer work at the church.

That's right, I was in town when Jesús came back to visit us. He had a bit of a reputation already, from the things he'd been doing in some of the coast towns, like Oxnard and Ventura. I was one of those young guys who didn't go to church much, except to go hang around outside the door of the church when there was a youth meeting, waiting for the girls who were there to come out. But when we heard that Jesús was going to talk at a prayer meeting, we went in to hear him.

The Book of Isaiah was given to him, and he opened it to the place where it says, "The Spirit of the Lord is upon me..."

They asked him to read from the Scriptures. He opened the Book and read – funny, I can still remember the words. I can't remember any other Scripture, but this still sticks in mind:
> "The Spirit of the Lord fills me,
> God has consecrated and blessed me and sent me.
> I come with a message of hope for the poor,
> To announce that prisoners will be released,
> That the blind will see,
> That the oppressed will be liberated.
> The day of God's blessing is here!"
Something about the way he read it made all of us sit up and pay attention – and remember it.

He closed the book and sat down. Everyone was looking at him. He said, "Today this Scripture is fulfilled as it reaches your ears."

Then he gave the book back to the secretary of the meeting, and he looked around at all of us. There was dead silence in that room. Everyone was looking at him. And he said, "You've heard it. The day is here!" And he talked about the coming reign of God and how now was the time to let God take over our lives and about how God loved everyone, even the people no one else could stand.

Everybody was real impressed at first about the way he talked. But after the meeting I heard a few people in the parking lot starting to mutter, "Who does he think he is? He's just a local kid who thinks he's a big shot now!"

Maybe he heard that, too, because at the next prayer meeting, the next week, he made a remark about how you've got to be from out of town to be called an expert – otherwise, even a prophet sent by God gets no respect. And then he talked some more about how God loved us all anyway, and God loved everybody – not just Americans, not just Mexicans, but Africans and Arabs and Chinese and everybody. He reminded people how in the Scriptures there are stories of God doing miracles for Arabs as well as Jews. He kept that up, week after week, every time they gave him a chance to talk.

Well, I kept going to hear him, but my buddies went back to hanging around in the parking lot till the meeting was over and their girl friends came out. And the older people were muttering more and more about the nerve of this guy, telling us we're no better than anyone else. It's a small town. Maybe we are no better than anyone else, but we don't like to be reminded of it. And some people were upset because they thought Mexicans were the enemy, and some people didn't like Arabs, or Jews, and some people thought he was selling out *la raza* by telling them to love Anglos. And then, some people were disappointed because they thought he was this big faith healer and he wasn't doing a lot of miracles in our town. So after a while there was lot of anger in the air.

One night after a prayer meeting just about everyone had left and Jesús came out into the parking lot and my old buddies are hanging around and they start giving him a hard time. Some of them have had a couple of beers, and they start pushing and shoving him. I was just watching from the door, you understand? I wasn't involved. But I thought maybe I should do something when they started pushing him toward the ravine behind the parking lot. Some guys – I'm not saying it was my friends – had thrown the Garcia kid in there a few months before, and he's still limping. They might have killed him. But all of a sudden Jesús just stops everything. Just stands there with all these crazy guys around him and looks at them. And they back off and look at the ground. And he just walks through the whole gang of them, and no one makes a move on him. When he goes by the door where I am, he looks at me and shakes his head – not mad, just real, real sad. I never saw him again.

Now, I'm not proud of me and my friends. But what was I supposed to do? And they wouldn't have acted like they did, even being young and drunk, if they hadn't thought the grown-ups in town would let them get away with it. You won't find many people here who'll admit it, but I say it's the whole town's fault that Jesús left us.

The said, "Is this not the son of Joseph?"

"No prophet is accepted in his own home territory… There were many widows in Israel in the days of Elias, but Elias was sent to a woman in foreign territory. There were sick people in Israel in the time of Elisha, but it was a Syrian whom he healed."

They were filled with anger.

They were going to throw him off the edge of the cliff on which the town was built. But he walked right through the middle of them all and went on his way.

And maybe it was just as well. He didn't come to a good end, did he? If he'd stayed here, we all would have had trouble with the Security Force. Better we should be left alone. But still, when I think of how he looked at me that night, I feel kind of sad myself.

[Would Jesus' message of love for enemies be welcomed in churches today? Do you think God loves the enemies of our country? Do you find it hard to love them? How often do any of us pray for those who hate us, in private or in public?]

NOTE TO SELF

[journal entry, inserted into notebook]

[Many scholars think that Luke's Gospel was written after Mark's, and is partly based on it.]

In my own journal I can be honest with myself. I'm not always doing original work here. After I'd already done some of my own research, I discovered that I'd been scooped by another brother who has written the story of Jesús in his own way.

His way is to tell a pretty bleak story of suffering and renunciation. I can understand that, given the tough times our people have seen, but there's more to Jesús' story than that. His way is also pretty terse: one anecdote after another, each told with as few words as possible, and not much about Jesús' teaching.

Question to self: how much of his work can I use without being guilty of plagiarism? It's a moral question, not a legal one. His work is not copyrighted. It's circulated by photocopies, of course, not formally published – who'd dare to publish it? He didn't even sign it. But still…

I guess I can use some of the framework he constructed -- that is, follow his outline. After all, I want to tell some of the same stories about Jesús – but also to flesh them out a bit, with some of my own research, where I can. Like in the story of Simon and his family.

SIMON'S WIFE

Luke 4:31-5:11

[partial transcript of an interview]

I first met Jesús through Simon.

We had been married a year. All through that year, Simon kept talking about his plans for the future. He and his buddies used to crew the boats that went out from the Harbor -- taking deep-sea sport fishermen out into the Channel. They were going to put all their money together and get a boat of their own. The trouble was, Simon had a big heart, and a big mouth, and he was always promising to do things for his friends, and then he couldn't follow through on his own projects. So he just kept talking about the boat business. Then he met Jesús and all of a sudden he was all Jesús this, Jesús that. So I told him, "Introduce me to this man you think is so great."

One evening he said to me, "Jesús is going to be talking at a meeting in the church hall – why don't you come?" That day, my mom, who was living with us, hadn't been feeling well, and I didn't want to leave her alone, but I didn't want to miss the opportunity, so I went with him.

We got there a little late. The hall was crowded. Jesús was talking, like he always did, about the coming reign of God, and God's healing power. Then this crazy man comes running down the aisle in the middle of the hall, shouting and waving his arms. I know every congregation has members who act crazy or get drunk sometimes, but this man was way beyond that. He was shouting things like, "You don't fool me, Jesús! I know who you are! Holy man, huh? Son of God, huh? Well, go back where you came from!" It was like the devil was in him – it scared me, bad, gave me the chills. But Jesús just looked at him and didn't even raise his voice, just said, calm but firm, "Stop it. Leave. Go on." And the man stopped and fell down in the middle of the floor. And then he sat up and shook himself and looked around like he had no idea where he was. And Jesús just gestured to him to take a seat, and went on talking. He talked about how there are some kinds of craziness and some kinds of evil that are beyond human control, and we have to face that, and trust in the power of God, and put our lives under the control of God's spirit.

I was really impressed. I nudged Simon and whispered, "Invite him over to the house!" And after the meeting was over he did come with us.

Luke 4:31-37

Jesus went to Capharnaum. He taught there in the meeting places. …

In the synagogue a man with an unholy spirit in him began shouting, "What are you doing to us? Killing us? I know who you are – the holy one from God!" Jesus reproached him. The demon threw the man down in the middle of them all, and left.

When we got home my mom was lying unconscious in her little bedroom in the back of the house. I felt her forehead and she was burning up. I went back out to the living room, crying: "I left my mother alone and now she's dying!" Then Jesús came back into the bedroom and touched her and said a word to her. And she sat up and looked at him and said, "Welcome to our humble *casita*. Let me put my robe on and I'll fix you something to eat. You must be hungry." That was my mom. After that, I was as big a fan as Simon.

Then Simon and his friends had a new idea. If Jesús would stay at our place, a lot of people would come around asking for favors, and somehow Simon could get them to help buy that boat. He might have pulled it off; he had a lot of charm and that gift of gab, which he had practiced on me already. But Jesús had other ideas, and bigger plans.

I wasn't too surprised when Simon and his friends decided they'd forget about boats and go on the road with Jesús. It was okay. I missed Simon, of course, but I knew what he was doing was important. He'd keep in touch by phone, from Lompoc or Bakersfield or wherever, but he only got home once in a while. I'd have gone with him, but someone had to hold a steady job and take care of mom.

Later, when he went to San Francisco, and then to Washington, I missed him even more. We'd exchange messages by e-mail, but he couldn't say too much about what he was doing, because the Security Force might intercept it. After my mother died, I waited a while, and then I went to Washington to join him. Rode all the way across the country by bus. The day I got there they arrested him.

I understood why they thought they had to do that, and even why they thought they had to execute him. But they didn't have to torture him. They didn't have to do that.

Or maybe they did. Maybe that's what's in their hearts and it has to come out somehow. But they're crazy if they think that will accomplish anything. The reign of God's Spirit can't be stopped. A lot of us older folks are gone now – dead or in jail. But you younger people are taking up the leadership and spreading the word. You are going to do that, aren't you?

[What's the worst thing you've had to endure in order to be true to your calling? Does the example of those who have put up with worse things inspire or encourage you?]

> From the synagogue, Jesus went to the house of Simon. Simon's mother-in-law had a high fever… Jesus told the fever to leave her, and it did. And she got up and served them.
>
> Luke 5:10-11 Simon and his friends, James and John, left their boats and followed Jesus.

WHO DOES HE THINK HE IS?
JESÚS STARTS TO ANNOY PEOPLE
Luke 5
[journal entries]

Simon's wife's question got to me. How could I give up this project now, after hearing this tough old lady talk like that? I went back to the cheap motel where I was staying, and reviewed my notes, and the pages photocopied from someone else's notes, and went back again the next day to talk to her some more.

I'm sorry to bother you, I said, but I've got these stories about Jesús, and I'm not sure what to make of them.

She looked over the pages I gave her and smiled, and said, these are about Jesús annoying people.

I don't get it, I said.

Well, for one thing, she said, people expected different things from him, and he didn't live up to what they wanted.

Like, some of them thought he was a faith healer, but he didn't put on a big show for them. When he was around, people got better, but he didn't make noise about it. Didn't shout or wave his arms or go on and on about how you'd be healed if you had faith. One time I watched him go up to some character on the street, some guy who was all broken down, maybe a needle-user, maybe had full-blown AIDS, wasn't taking care of himself, looked awful, smelled worse, and Jesús went up and put his arm around his shoulders and talked to him quietly for a couple of minutes, and then said, "Go to a clinic and get checked. And take care of yourself." A week later the guy came through my supermarket checkout stand looking like he'd never seen a bad day in his life. And telling everyone in the checkout line what Jesús had done for him. But Jesús didn't want publicity. Still, some people thought he should have been more like a traditional faith healer.

Then there were people who thought he made too much of himself. Some of them thought that they should have control of what went on in the name of God. I was at a talk he gave in the grand meeting room of our one big hotel. It was standing room only – if you got there late, you couldn't get in. There were a bunch of clergy and theologians sitting in the front row, looking skeptical. Jesús was talking, like always, about what it would mean if we let God run the world. Then there was this big racket and tiles start falling down from the ceiling. Seems some people had brought a friend of theirs who was what do you call it, paraplegic, and when they couldn't get in the door

Luke 5:12-26

A man with leprosy begged Jesus to heal him. "If you will, you can cleanse me." Jesus stretched out his hand and touched him and said, "I will. Be cleansed." Immediately he was healed. Jesus told him not to tell anyone else except the religious authorities who could certify him as "clean".

One day he was teaching, and some traditional religious leaders and experts in religious law had come from various places to hear him…

Some men brought a paralyzed patient on a stretcher, but they could not get into the place where Jesus was because of the crowd, so they carried him up to the roof and let him down through the ceiling. Jesus said, "Your sins are forgiven." Then, seeing how upset the religious leaders were, he said, ".....get up and take your stretcher and go home."

5:36-37 "No one patches an old coat with new cloth, or puts new wine into old wineskins."

they hauled him up into the crawl space under the roof – you know, where the air conditioning ducts are – and if they hadn't had ropes around him he would have been killed falling through the ceiling. As it was, he was just lying there on the floor in the front of the auditorium, looking dazed. The first thing Jesús said was, "It's okay. You're forgiven. I mean, you're forgiven everything. Your life starts over, now."

The men in the front row started muttering to each other and glaring at Jesús. Jesús looked hard at them for a minute. He said, "You think I'm going too far, don't you? How about this?" And he said to the man on the floor, "Get up. Go home. But don't forget the wheelchair your friends left outside – you can push it home by yourself now."

And the man got up and walked out.

Well, the guys in the front row just about had a fit. Sometimes it seemed like he was deliberately getting in their faces, showing them up.

Then there were the pious traditional folks who thought Jesús should be pious and traditional, too, and follow their practices and devotions. Not bad things, but some of them were really stuck in their ways. They'd say, "We've always done things this way." And they'd criticize Jesús for not following them. And Jesús would say things like, "There's a new day dawning! There's a new world being made! Some folks are like old rusty containers – try to put something new in them and they just bust at the seams. Well, I'm something new, and I'm looking for a new kind of people, and I'm not going to be stopped by the way you've always done things."

You had to figure, either he's crazy, or he's really something else.

[What do you make of the real Jesus of Nazareth? What do you expect of him?]

THE CORE GROUP

Luke 5:27; 6:12-16; 8:1-3; 9:1-7

[scribblings in notebook]……

Luke 6:12-16

After spending the night in prayer, Jesus called his "disciples" to him, and chose twelve, whom he called "apostles." They were Simon, whom he called Peter, and Andrew his brother, and James and John, Philip and Bartholomew, Matthew and Thomas, James son of Alphaeus, and Simon called "the Zealot", and Judas Iscariot, the traitor.

[The twelve are thought to represent the twelve ancestors of the twelve tribes of ancient Israel.]

I have some bits and pieces of information about the close followers of Jesús. I'm not sure how to put them all together.

In some of the stories, it's hard to tell when Jesús was being serious with them, and when he was being playful, and when he was both at once.

At a certain point he apparently realized that he wasn't having a lot of success trying to reach whole crowds of people at once. People would listen, and be impressed, but they wouldn't change their minds, or their hearts, or their lives. So I guess he decided to concentrate on a smaller inner circle of followers.

To begin with, they didn't call themselves "followers" but learners, *discípulos*. They were more like a school than a political movement. But there was no doubt about who was the teacher – and the leader.

He must have given this development a lot of thought and prayer. They say he did that before any serious decision. Then he chose a sort of core group of thirteen "missionaries," as Jesús called them.

I have a list of their names, but I haven't been able to track any of them down – they're either dead, or disappeared. Most of the names appear to be Latino, though some sound Anglo. They could be African American or Asian American. It's hard to imagine a group in California that wouldn't be pretty diverse. On the other hand, Jesús talked a lot about *nosotros*, and focused his early efforts on "our people." I need to do more research on this.

He was serious about their mission; he sent them out to talk about the coming reign of God, and to make the talk real for people by helping them with their immediate needs. But he didn't let them take themselves too seriously.

"Why just thirteen?" one asked him. "I don't get it."

"It's a symbol," said Jesús. "There were thirteen states in the original United States of America, thirteen stars in the flag. We're about renewing the nation, making a fresh start. So, I've chosen thirteen stars."

"Symbolic, huh? I don't think anyone will get it."

"Smart people will get it," said Jesús, silencing the questioner.

Then there were the nicknames. Like "Pedro" for Simon. "Your head's like a *piedra,* a stone," Jesús told him. "I can't pound anything into it. But I need you to be a rock – for me and for your brothers and sisters."

There was another Simon, who got nicknamed "the Militant." This was at a time when being called "militant" had been un-cool for decades. It sounded like this Simon was stuck in a time warp. (Could it be that nickname wasn't given by Jesús, but by some later list-maker, at a time when it was again fashionable to be a "militant"? Another issue for further research.)

Then there's the question of the women who were close to Jesús. There were women who worked with him, traveled with him, and kept things going when the men faltered. I've got some of their names, too – Susana, Joanne C., Mary M., and others. But the list of the Thirteen Missionaries includes only men. Why? Jesús is reported to have said, "They're my homeboys, my posse." Since Jesús was nothing like the kind of thugs who usually have homeboys or a posse, no one could take that explanation seriously. But I have no other explanation from Jesús. (More research?)

And I can't forget the story of the IRS agent. It seems that Jesús and a bunch of his hangers-on were standing on the sidewalk outside a building where the IRS had a local office. One of the group was going on, loud and long, about the evils of that organization: how the government used the agents to harass those it didn't like, how the agents abused their power to extort money from people, and so on. Just at this moment one of the agents comes out the door. As it happens, he's Latino, and the haranguer raises his voice about how "some of our own people have sold out to the system like traitors."

Now the agent is a desk jockey, not an enforcer, and all he wants is to sidle past this group and get to his car. But just as he opens the car door, Jesús points at him, and calls out, "Hey, friend! Come with me." And he walks off down the street, and the man follows him. What did they talk about? I don't know.

But that evening the agent, now a former agent, invites Jesús to his condo for pizza, and to meet some of his friends, most of whom

---

Luke 8:1-3
Jesus went through one town after another, talking about the reign of God, along with the twelve, as well as several women: Mary Magdalen, Joanna, Susanna, and many others...

Luke 5:27-39

Jesus saw a tax collector named Levi and said, "Follow me." And he left everything and followed him.

Levi gave a dinner party for Jesus at his house.

also work for the IRS. And Jesús brings along some people he knows, including some former drug addicts and drunks and hookers. ("Former" meaning, in this context, clean and sober for at least a few days.) I can imagine the bureaucrats and the low-lifes sitting around sharing pizza and trying to be polite to each other, and Jesús, the only one in the room who's comfortable, having a fine time.

Eventually, it seems that this agent became one of Jesús' core group.

> **"I did not come to call the righteous, but sinners."**

Jesús took a lot of flak for this kind of thing. The politically correct didn't think he should have anything to do with IRS agents. Some pious folks didn't like his hanging around with lowlifes. Jesús shrugged the criticism off. "If some folks have their act together," he said, "they don't need me. I'm a healer for those who realize they're sick."

So what does all this mean? That Jesús had a lot of charm, that he could change someone's life with a gesture and a word? That he liked pizza? That he enjoyed annoying both the politically correct and religiously righteous? Maybe all of the above.

[Who do you suppose would be in a core group of Jesus' followers nowadays? Could you imagine yourself among them? Would you be comfortable with the others?]

NOTE TO SELF (2): Q & A
Luke 6:17
[journal entry]

Someone who knew of my research gave me a paper and I stuck it in the back of my notebook and got around to reading it days later. When I realized what it was, I couldn't remember who had given it to me. It might be really important.

After all, we have no videotapes, no live recordings of what Jesús said in his public speeches. The Security Force was quite efficient and effective when they decided to destroy all such things. But here I have a computer printout from an old web site with quotations of his words by people who claim they heard him speak. It seems that before Security clamped down on the Web, there was a kind of cyber-community of followers of Jesús who would post remembered sayings of his on their web site. They had to keep changing the URL and switching servers, until eventually Security caught up with them and shut it down.

Meanwhile, they built up quite a collection of "sayings of Jesús." Some are humorous, some are cynical, some are challenging, some are grim. (Did the tone of the postings change, I wonder, as things got tougher for the members of the community?)

There was a stereotyped format that the web site users followed. It went like this:

Q.: What did Jesús say about religious hypocrites?
A.: Jesús said, "How come you can see the speck in your brother's eye, and not the board in your own? Get the board out your own eye, and then you can see enough to help your brother."

Q.: What did Jesús say about people who criticized him?
A.: Jesús said, "You can badmouth me all you want, but don't attack the work of God's Spirit. That's unforgivable."

Q.: What did Jesús say about the rich and the poor?
A.: Jesús said, "God blesses you who are poor, but God help you who are rich!"

Q.: What did Jesús <u>really</u> say about the rich and the poor?
A.: Jesús really said, "Up with the poor! Down with the rich!"

Webmaster's note: all right, you guys, quit posting things you wish Jesús had said, or what you suspect he would have said if only he'd thought of it! This is supposed to be a serious site. Keep it up, and you'll be banned from the site.

[Many scholars think that Luke's Gospel makes use of a collection of sayings of Jesus that already had been written down.
They call this the Quelle (German for Source) or simply Q Document. Some think they can detect earlier and later additions to this collection of sayings.
Whatever the real Luke had before him when he wrote, I can imagine my imaginary "Luke" coming across such a document.]

Now what should I do with this stuff? It is, or was, placed in the public domain, so there's no question of plagiarism. But can I trust it? Of course it's a very selective sample of Jesús' teachings, reflecting the interests of the people who liked to post things on the Web. But how can I be sure Jesús really said the things they put in his mouth? What if some of them just made things up? I've got to go back to Ventura County and talk with people I know heard him speak.

JESÚS, THE RICH AND THE POOR

Luke 6:20-38

[journal entry]

Luke 6:17-26

Looking at his disciples, Jesus said:
"Blessed the poor—yours is the kingdom of God.
Blessed those now hungry – You will be filled.
Blessed those now crying – you will laugh.
Blessed are you when people hate and reject and ostracize you because of the Savior…
Your reward will be great in heaven…
But woe to you, the rich, for you have your comfort now.
Woe to you who are full, for you will be hungry.
Woe to you who laugh now, for you will weep.
Woe to you if everyone speaks well of you – that is how people have always treated false prophets.
But love your enemies, do good to those who hate you, bless those who persecute you. If hit on one cheek, turn the other."

I found the old man in a farm worker village near Saticoy, just a few miles east -- that is, inland -- from Ventura. In the early evening, he was sitting in the back yard of his modest home, where there was just room for a table and a few chairs. Though old enough to be retired, he was dressed as a *campesino*: denim shirt and jeans, work boots, and a broad brimmed hat. He offered me a drink from the six-pack on the table; I didn't care for his brand of Mexican beer, but accepted it out of politeness. While we were still exchanging small talk, his son came by for a visit. The son, a little older than me, wore suit and tie – he was coming from his office in Ventura, he explained.

"I was just about to ask your father if he'd ever heard Jesús talk about rich and poor people. You know some people say he was down on the rich…"

"Of course I heard him," the old man said. "He said, 'Down with the rich! Up with the poor!' You remember, too, *m'ijo*, don't you. You were a little boy, but not too little to go to rallies with me."

"Yes, I remember hearing him speak, but I don't remember him saying 'Down with the rich!' He didn't hate anybody."

"I remember," said the older man, not to be deterred, "when Jesús came here and talked to us in the open field in the middle of this village. It was a hot summer night, a beautiful night, the kind when all the fruit trees in the valley are filling the air with a sweet smell, and the moon was all the light we had or needed for our meeting. That was a hard time, an angry time: workers were striking all over the county and the owners were doing everything to keep us in our place.

"Jesús said, 'Most of you are poor. Many of you have reason to feel bad. Some of you are hungry. A few of you have been arrested and beaten up. You have to remember that God is on your side. God loves you. God blesses you. When God's love rules the world, things will be different. But you can't hate people, and you can't use violence to get what you need. When they hit you, you have to take it, and keep on doing what's right."

[Note: Luke's presentation of Jesus' teaching is a little different from the more famous version of the Beatitudes in Matthew 5:1-12.]

Luke 16:19-31: The story of the rich man and Lazarus

I broke in. "Was he saying all this in English?" I wanted to know what Jesús' exact words were. But the old man said, no, Jesús was speaking Spanish because that was what most of the crowd understood. My own Spanish wasn't good enough to follow a speech in that language, so I had to settle for the old man's version of Jesús' talk and hope he was giving me the gist of it correctly.

"He made us feel like we had dignity," the old man went on. "Here was this man, who was getting to be famous, and he came and sat down with us and shared our poor supper. He respected everyone and treated everyone like they were important."

The son came in to the conversation again: "You see, he didn't say hate the rich. He just wanted them to treat the poor people right."

The father shook his head and snorted, "You young people are too busy trying to get ahead to understand what Jesús was telling us. He was poor himself, he didn't have much of anything, and he could have – he could have been a rich preacher on TV. But he spent his time helping other people. If everyone acted like that, instead of trying to make money for themselves, the world would be different."

"But look at me!" the younger man protested. "I'm not rich, but I've got a decent job, so I can help you out and you don't have to work any more. Is that so bad?"

"What about Jesús' story of the rich man and the homeless man?" asked the father, avoiding his son's question. "The rich man ignores the poor one, and when they die, who goes to heaven and who goes to hell? You remember the story."

The son seemed to give up on his father and turned to me. "I think," he said, "that Jesús meant that we should be spiritually poor. We should realize that we're all poor in God's eyes. We should have compassion for people who are suffering. We should share what we've got with people who are hungry. But I don't think he was *against* anyone."

They were both looking at me now. I didn't want to get into what I suspected was a long running argument between father and son. Besides, it was getting late. And the father, having put away a couple of the beers he'd offered me, was looking a little sleepy. I just said, "It sounds to me like Jesús did say some pretty radical things. I guess his followers will be arguing about what to make of them for a while yet. Even when we know what he meant, we may not be able to live up to his vision of the world."

I thanked them and got up to go. The older man was still muttering, "He did say the poor are blessed. He didn't say the rich are blessed."

The younger man was repeating, "You can be poor, in a way, without being broke."

As I drove away, through the moonlit, citrus-fragrant night, I tried to imagine Jesús and the crowd of really poor, long-suffering workers gathered around him on that night long ago, and his voice reaching out to touch their hearts. All I could think was, "Jesús 'followers' don't all do such a great job of following. But maybe it's better to be a confused, stumbling follower of his than no follower at all."

[Many people have found the words of Jesus as reported by the Gospel according to Luke too harsh, and have tried to soften them in one way or another. The story above tries to put them in a near-contemporary context where they fit, and offers three different responses to the challenge. Who do you think would be the "rich" and the "poor" in our world? Where do you fit in? How do you deal with the challenging words of Jesus?]

THE COLONEL'S AIDE AND THE WIDOW'S SON
Luke 7:1-17
[stories typed by author and inserted in notebook]

Luke 7:1-10

There was a Roman officer who had a servant who was ill. The servant was important to him. He sent elders from among the Jews to Jesus, asking him to come and save the servant. They said, "He deserves it. He's friendly to our people and has built a synagogue for us."

But when Jesus was close to his home, he sent friends to say, "Don't trouble yourself. I am not worthy to have you come under my roof. Just say a word, and my servant will get better. I am a person of authority, too; when I tell someone to do something, he does it."

I have these anecdotes, in sketchy form, one from what I think of as my usually reliable source – those photocopied pages – and the other from another source. But they seem to go together. Here is how I imagine them playing out in reality.

Jesús had taken the bus to Santa Barbara. No sooner did he get off the bus than he was surrounded by "friends" who had come to talk to him. They all wanted favors: help me get my uncle out of jail, have you got a job for my cousin, can you help me organize a rally, will you give a talk at this fund-raiser I'm planning. They followed him out into the parking lot, Jesús listening and not saying much.

Into the parking lot came a big black van, very official looking. Almost all of Jesús' "friends" scatter, figuring that this is the Security Force come to arrest Jesús and them too. But it turns out the driver is a civilian, and alone.

This driver says to Jesús, "*Desculpe la molestia*, excuse the trouble, but I've come to ask a favor. There's a Colonel Smith here in town – this van is from his headquarters – and yes, he's an Anglo, and he's Security, and that's supposed to make him a bad guy, but really, he's okay – he's friendly to us, gives a lot of money to local charities, and so on. Well, the point is, one of his aides, a lieutenant, a kid he was mentoring, has been diagnosed with leukemia. The doctors don't have much hope for him. The colonel knew you were coming to town – he's SecForce, they know everything that's going on – and he asked me to drive down here and ask if you could do something."

Jesús asks the obvious question, "And who are you?"

"Just a friend of the colonel," says the man. "He's done me a few favors, and I've done a few for him. This one I owe him. Can you help?"

Jesús thinks a minute, says, "Okay," and gets in the van.

Then the driver's cell phone rings and he picks it up and listens for a minute. He turns to Jesús and says, "It's the Colonel. He doesn't expect you to come personally. He knows what you might think of him, being who and what he is. But he's a Colonel, and he's used to saying jump and people asking how high. And he figures you must be at least a Colonel in God's organization – so could you just say a word for the benefit of his aide?"

Jesus said, "I have not found this much faith among the people of Israel."

Jesús looks at him, and looks around at the almost empty parking lot, and looks back into the bus station, where some of his "friends" are hiding, and laughs. "Sounds like this guy has more faith in me than my own people do."

He takes the phone and says, "Colonel Smith? It's going to be all right. The young man's going to recover…No problem. And thanks for your confidence in me."

After that Jesús goes around town trying to meet with different groups of people. But everywhere he goes, the van shows up too.

"It's the colonel's way of saying thanks," the driver explains. "He asked me to keep an eye on you. *Si cualquier cosa se le ofrece*, I'm at your service."

But the result is that few people come around where Jesús goes, because they don't want to get near that van.

"Clever man, that colonel," says Jesús. "He shows gratitude and at the same time he keeps me from stirring up trouble."

"I never thought you came to town to make trouble," protests the driver.

"No, but what does your colonel think?" says Jesús. "You might as well give me a ride back down south."

They start down the 101 but only get as far as Carpinteria when a red emergency vehicle goes screaming by. "Paramedics," says Jesús, "Follow them. I've got a hunch…"

The driver is unhappy about it but manages to make the freeway exit and get on a surface street in time to see the paramedics turn onto a side street. He follows them into what looks like a quiet little neighborhood of modest homes. In the third block there's a small crowd gathered. By the time Jesús and the driver get there, the paramedics are standing around the body of a boy lying in the street. They're just shaking their heads.

A woman is kneeling by the boy's body. She's rocking back and forth, crying, "My baby, my baby! First my husband, now my boy. This is horrible. Horrible! Horrible!"

"Poor kid," one of the small crowd of neighbors says. "Riding his bike, and he fell, and hit his head on the curb."

Luke 7:11-17

While he was going to a town called Naim… the only son of a mother who was a widow was being carried out, dead. Jesus felt deep compassion for her, and said., "Don't cry." He went up and touched the stretcher and said, "Young man, get up." The dead man sat up and began to talk. Jesus gave him back to his mother.

"Probably died before the wheels stopped turning," said another. "At least he didn't suffer."

"Should have been wearing a helmet," says another.

The mother of the boy just kneels there in the street, crying.

The paramedics lift the body of the boy onto a stretcher and raise it to put it into their vehicle. But Jesús steps forward and says, "Hold it there, please."

The paramedics look at him funny, but after all, he did get out of that big black van, so they stop.

Jesús says to the little boy, "Hey, *hermanito,* what are you lying there for? Get up, your mother needs you."

The boy sits up and says, "Where's my mom?"

Jesús gestures toward her and the boy slides off the stretcher and runs to her. "Why are you crying, mama?"

The paramedics and the neighbors just stand there with their mouths open.

Jesús looks at the driver and his look says, "If we don't get out of here before these folks catch their breath, they'll never let us go." The driver gets it and they head for the van and back to the freeway.

But Jesús' look also said, "You see? I don't do favors just for people who do favors for me."

The driver might not have got that part of it.

[What do you need Jesus to do for you? Do you think he can do it?]

JESÚS AND JOHN, ONCE AGAIN

Luke 5:33; 7:18-35; 9:1-7

[photocopy of newspaper article, with comment]

CO-CONSPIRATORS INDICTED

Indictments were handed down today against two more dissidents accused of co-operating in the activities of the recently executed felon known as "John". Specifically, they were charged with smuggling information to him and from him when he was in prison, and so enabling him to communicate with other subversives.

The accused have shown no remorse. Given an opportunity to do so, one launched into a verbal attack on the prosecutors. "You political types," he shouted, "bend with the wind. You sell your souls so you can have big offices and wear expensive suits. John was just the opposite, and people traveled miles to see him, but no one would cross the street for you!"

Both of those indicted admitted continued commitment to radical revolution. "We expect someone to finish what John started," one stated. "And not someone like Jesús. We're looking for someone who'll change things, fast, not a nice guy who does favors for sick people. Not that you fools can tell the difference. John and his folks are lean and mean, and you arrest us; Jesús and his friends like parties, and sooner or later you'll go after them!"

The prosecutor affirmed confidence that convictions would follow quickly, given the attitude and the words of the accused.

Governor Herrold's office issued a statement of the Governor's satisfaction with the process of justice in this case. "As for the one known as Jesús," the statement said, "it is not yet clear that

---

Luke 5:33-34:

"John's disciples fast and pray; why don't yours?"

Luke 7:18-35:

John's disciples told him about Jesus' activities. He sent two of them to Jesus to ask, "Are you the one who is to come, or do we still have to wait for someone else?" Jesus was curing many sick and blind and troubled people. He told John's men, "Go tell John what you've witnessed – people are being healed, and the poor are getting good news. Blessed is the one who isn't turned off by me!"

Jesus said about John: "Why did you all go out into the desert to see John? Because he was like a desert reed that bends with every wind? Because he was so well dressed? Those kinds of people are in the royal palace, not in the dungeons. .. John was the greatest man of his time… But public opinion nowadays makes me think of a bunch of children who complain no matter what is offered them. John fasted; I eat; we both get criticized."

Luke 9:9

Herod: "Who is this Jesus I hear so much about?"

he is not part of the web of conspiracy.
Our investigation is ongoing."

I was surprised when someone handed this to me: first, because so little material has survived the work of the Security Force; and second, because Jesús spoke so well of John/Juan, according to that Q&A document. Maybe what's reported here reflects the opinions of the speakers, rather than of John. Or maybe it reflects journalistic imagination.

[In what ways does Jesus disappoint people's hopes and expectations? In what ways does he disappoint yours?]

ETIQUETTE
Luke 7:36-50
[journal entry]

Luke 7:36-50

**One of the religious conservatives invited him to a dinner…
A woman in the town who was a sinner, finding out that he was there, brought a jar of ointment and began to wash his feet with her tears and dry them with her hair. She kissed his feet and rubbed them with the ointment.**

One of the things I like about doing this research is that it brings me into contact with a lot of older people. They're mellow, they're thoughtful, and they have interesting stories to tell. Like this one, from a nice old lady in Santa Barbara. To look at her, you'd think she never did anything more scandalous than disco dancing. But here's what she told me.

"When I was young, I used to work in a strip joint. For a few extra bucks, I'd do a lap dance for a customer, and for more money, I'd do more. Eventually it dawned on me that I was putting my health and safety at risk, so I quit.

"But then I went back to it. I got arrested in a sting operation by the vice squad, and got my picture in the paper, and became a bit of a local celebrity. But after I did some jail time, I said, enough, I'm quitting for good.

"Only I couldn't. I made all kinds of good resolutions, and broke them all. I'd get beat up by some guy, and swear that I was going to clean up my life, and a few weeks or months later, I'd say, well, I can make a little money and will be all right this time – and it never was. You know how they say, insanity is doing the same thing over and over and expecting different results. That was my life.

"It was like an addiction. I knew it was sick. I knew I was sick. So I heard about this man named Jesús and how he healed people. He came to town more than once, and I'd go to hear him talk, but he didn't seem like your standard faith healer, and I didn't have the nerve to go up and ask him if he could cure me of my craziness.

"But finally I couldn't stand it any more, couldn't stand myself any more, and the next time Jesús was in town I tracked him down – at a party. It seems like this guy named Simon something-or-other – I knew his name, but it won't come to me now. Anyhow this Simon what's-his-name was having a kind of radical chic party at his big house in Montecito. You know, invite his friends, and invite this controversial character, show how broad-minded he is, in spite of being one of the pillars of the church locally.

"Well, I crashed the party. Just waltzed in past the guys at the door and into the big room where they're serving cocktails and little

> The host said to himself: if this man were a prophet, he would know that the woman who's all over him is a sinner. Jesus said: Simon… there were once two debtors; one owed lots of money and the other a little. Both were forgiven their debt by their creditor. Which would love him more? Simon: I suppose, the one who got the bigger write-off. Jesus said, "You have given the right answer. … Do you see this woman? When I entered your house, you did not extend to me the signs of welcome customary in our culture: a kiss, water for washing my feet, anointing oil – but she has washed my feet and kissed them and anointed them. A lot of sins are forgiven her, for she has shown a lot of love. Small forgiveness goes with small love. To the woman Jesus said: Your sins are forgiven… Your faith has saved you. Go, to a life of peace."

things on crackers. And there off to one side of the room was Jesús, sort of by himself.

"I lost it then. I just went up and threw myself at his feet and grabbed him around the knees and started bawling. I knew I was making an awful fool of myself but I couldn't stop. I mean, that's not how one is supposed to behave at a high-class party, is it? I suppose everyone in the room was staring.

"But this Simon knew who I was. For that matter, I knew him. – How did I know him? How do you think? – And he must have said something or given a look, because Jesús started in on him.

" 'Simon,' he said, 'Let me tell you a story. There was a woman who overdrew her checking account at the local bank by fifty dollars. There was also a man who got way, way behind on his mortgage payments. The bank manager knew them both and arranged it so both of them got lots of time to set things right. Now who had a better reason to consider the bank manager a friend?'

"Simon, bright lad that he was, said, 'The one who got the bigger deal.'

Jesús said, 'You got that right. Now let's talk about proper behavior. You invited me to your house, didn't you? But once I got here, you gave me a cold eye and a cold handshake and have been avoiding talking to me all evening. You want to impress your guests by having me at your party, but you don't want them to think we're friends, or anything like that. But take this woman here… She's not afraid to be close to me. She's not ashamed to be my friend.'

"He took me by the hand and lifted me to my feet. 'Your life has been out of control,' he said. 'But you didn't give up. And you were willing to do whatever you had to do to get straightened out. From now on, you don't have to keep making yourself miserable. And you don't have to hang around this party any longer, if you don't want to. It's not much fun, anyway.'

She paused, and then went on. "He was right. I didn't have to keep beating myself up." Another pause.

"You remember I said Jesús wasn't like your typical faith healer. He didn't have to be. Just walking into a room, he brought the healing power of God with him. And just by being around him you'd be better off. If you wanted to be."

[Have you experienced psychological or emotional healing by Jesus?]

43

IMAGES
Luke 8:4-18

[reflections in notebook]

> **Luke 8:4-14**
>
> **As crowds gathered around him, Jesus told this parable: The sower went out to sow the seed. Some fell along the path way and was stepped on and eaten by birds. Some fell on rock and dried up as it sprouted. Some fell where the growth was choked by thorns. But some fell on good ground and grew up to produce a hundredfold. Let whoever has ears, Listen! When his disciples asked him about the parable, he told them: To you is given knowledge of the Kingdom of God..."**

It seems that Jesús often told stories or used images in talking to people. A lot of these have been written down and retold. Some people find them strange, or puzzling. In real life, people don't do the kinds of things they do in his stories. But God does. It seems to me many of the stories are pretty straightforward, if you think about the situation in which Jesús spoke.

Take, for example, his image of the woman with the back-yard garden. She didn't have much luck. Gravel in the soil, or weeds, or raids by the neighbors' dog, or kids running though the yard did in most of what she planted. But a few things flourished, and she had lots of tomatoes and zucchini to share with her friends and relatives – more than she could give away, maybe.

Now, think about the situation. John had said someone would come along to finish what he started, and God would rule the world. But John, or at least some of his followers, had gotten pretty impatient with the slow results of Jesús' activity. And it's easy to imagine Jesús' own company of "learners" grumbling, "Where is this Kingdom of God he talks about? The bad guys still seem to be running things." And then Jesús himself could see what was happening: some people wouldn't listen to him at all, some had a big conversion experience and forgot it a week later, and some followed him for a while and then got thinking about their careers and left.

The image of the gardener would have reminded his community of "learners" that God does rule over our history. Even the rejection and the backsliding would somehow fit into God's plan. And the people who did grow and flourish spiritually, though few, made the work of planting seeds worthwhile. Or, to put it differently, someday the small fires he was lighting would blaze up to be seen by the whole world.

Still, I suppose the indifferent responses he often got hurt him. And as time went on, he concentrated more and more on conversations with the few, and let the many get what they could out of his public talks.

[Do you get impatient with the pace of progress? If so, how do you deal with your own impatience?]

TROUBLES
Luke 8-9
[notes in notebook]

Luke 8:40-56 Jesus heals the daughter of Jairus and a woman with a hemorrhage.

Luke 8:19-21 His mother and his brothers came to see him. "My mother and my brothers are those who listen to God's word and act on it."

Whatever else was going on, Jesús continued to show the greatest compassion toward people who really needed and wanted his help. A little girl on her deathbed, a woman who had been chronically ill for years – he was all kindness toward them.

Though he was concentrating more on his inner circle, Jesús still made efforts to reach larger numbers of people. But he sometimes had trouble with people misunderstanding him.

His own relatives and childhood friends, who had not been of much help to him when he visited his home town, would sometimes show up at his public appearances and act as if they had a special claim on him. If he was doing so much for other people, why couldn't he do extra favors for them? Even better, why couldn't he let them handle the business end of his work and get a cut of the income that would flow from a properly organized ministry? He might insist, "My family, now, is the community of those who pursue the word and will of God," but it's not clear how many of his relatives grasped that.

[Is it more common now than in Jesus' day to consider ourselves closely connected to those who are not our own flesh and blood? Whom do you count as 'family,' and sincerely call 'brothers' and 'sisters'? Do you consider yourself part of Jesus' family?]

MORE TROUBLES
Luke 8:26-39
[further notes]

Luke 8:26-39

They went by boat to the territory of the Gerasenes, on the other side of the Sea of Galilee. There was a man filled with demons…

When Jesus asked his name, the man said, "Legion."

There was a herd of pigs there, and the demons asked to be allowed to enter the pigs. The herd ran off a cliff and drowned. The people from the town asked Jesus to go away. The man who'd been freed wanted to go with Jesus, but Jesus told him to go home.

Strangers could be as bad or worse. Once, I was told, he made a foray up the coast toward Cayucos. He and his companions drove up and pulled into a parking lot outside of town, on a bluff overlooking the ocean. It happened to be the gathering place of a motorcycle club. They had parked their big machines, the kind they call "hogs," left the motors running, and were standing around in the parking lot drinking beer and telling each other stories of their exploits. Suddenly one of them started screaming and falling down and banging his head on the asphalt. Then he pulled a chain off his belt and started swinging it around, and everyone jumped back out of the way.

"Don't mind him," one of the bikers said. "He does that all the time. Too much LSD when he was younger, I guess."

"It ain't LSD," said another. "It's the evil in him."

Jesús approached the madman and asked, "Who are you?"

"They call me Fourth Division!" the man screamed. The Fourth Division was, of course, headquartered in Los Angeles, but garrisons were stationed throughout the Southern California Military District.

Jesús said, "You don't look like one of General Pilato's men."

"I'm not *one* of them! I'm a whole army! And you don't need to tell us who you are! You've come to torture us! All we want is our hogs and our beer!"

"Forget about the beer," said Jesús, "but you can have the hogs."

The man who told me this story swore by his tattoo that the motorcycles suddenly shifted into gear of their own accord and roared off the bluff and into the ocean. Then the crazy man got up and stood there calmly smiling. The rest of the motorcycle gang were too scared to do attack Jesús but suggested he'd better get out of town. The wild man, no longer wild, wanted to go with Jesús, wherever he was going – but Jesús said he'd spent too much of his life on the road – he should go home and tell people what God had done for him.

[How do we deal with "crazy" people today? How should we?]

A PICNIC BY THE LAKE
Luke 9:10-17
[still more notes]

Luke 9:10-17

A crowd followed Jesus to a deserted area by the lake. The Twelve said: Send them away so they can get some food. Jesus said: Feed them yourselves. They said: All we have are five loaves and two fishes. Jesus blessed the loaves and fishes, and the crowd ate till they were satisfied.

There's another story about a whole crowd who were fed. This seems to be one of the favorite stories of Jesús' followers. As they tell it, Jesús was up in the Santa Ynez Valley by Lake Cachuma talking to people in a park by the lakeside, and people kept coming and coming until there were hundreds of them – some say thousands. It got later and later but no one wanted to leave. Finally someone from the core group pointed out to Jesús, "These folks never get enough to eat, and now they're going to be stuck out here with no place to get supper. We better tell them to go."

Jesús said, "Better you should give them supper yourselves."

"With what? We didn't even bring enough for ourselves. Just enough for a few fish sandwiches."

But Jesús had them organize the crowd and said a blessing over the bread and broke it into pieces and had them start distributing it.

Nobody went away hungry, they say.

Now I've heard people listen to that story and say it shows how Jesús could inspire people to share what they had with each other. But those who told the story meant to say that this was a real miracle.

So what's the problem? It's not that people didn't appreciate the free picnic. They did. But most of them did not appreciate its meaning. They wanted more free food, naturally, but not more nourishment for their souls

[What is the connection in Jesus' ministry between caring for people's material needs and their spiritual needs? How could we imitate his actions today?]

SIMON: AS TOLD BY HIS WIFE
Luke 9: 18-21
[notes from a conversation]

[Note: Mark's Gospel does present the disciples this .]

Luke 9:18-21:

Once when Jesus was alone with his disciples, he asked them, "Who do people say I am?"
They said, "John the Baptist, or Elijah, or one of the ancient prophets."
He asked them, "Who do you say I am?"

Peter answered, "The Christ, the Anointed One, from God."

But Jesus warned them not to tell that to anyone.

Jesús' own inner circle often misunderstood him. According to my usually reliable source, his core group constantly missed the point of what he was saying and doing. They seemed to need a book like "Discipleship for Dummies" or "The Idiot's Guide to Liberation." I wonder if they were really that out of it. Maybe I should go back and talk to Simon's wife again…

…

She was quite willing to talk with me, but she seemed unwell, and I wondered if this might be my last visit with her. I was anxious to find out how she saw her husband's understanding of Jesús.

"I'll tell you," she said, "about a scene Simon described to me. I don't think he was supposed to talk about it, but he wasn't very good at keeping quiet.

"Jesús and company were camping out at the beach near Point Sal. Ever been there? It's beautiful – a big broad stretch of white sand, with cliffs on one side, and the ocean on the other – cold blue-green breakers coming in one after another. It was evening, and there were a few clouds in the sky, and they were waiting to see the sunset over the water.

"They'd been sitting around talking about the buzz on Jesús. You know, up and down the coast, there was a lot of talk, just like now. If you dared to take a poll, you might get something like: 30% say he's another Juan, 30% say he's Emiliano Zapata come back to life, 30% vote for Jeremiah from ancient times, and 10% don't know or don't care. All of a sudden Jesús says to them, 'And what do you think of me?'

"He says it kind if casually but they all know it's a terribly important question to him, and for them, too. Nobody says anything for a minute. Then Simon, who else, says, 'You're the Liberator sent by God!'

"There's another minute of silence while Jesús looks at Simon. Then he tells Simon, 'Don't use that word in public. People will expect me to be leading a charge on Pilato's headquarters with a flag in one hand and an AK-47 in the other. That's not me, and you know it. But how do you think the Security Force would react if they heard me calling myself "Liberator"?

He said, "The Son of Man has to suffer much and be condemned by the elders and chief priests and scribes -- and after three days, rise again." He added, "If anyone wants to follow me, let him take up his cross…"

Luke 9:23-24 "Anyone who wishes to follow me must renounce self… Those who give their lives for me will save themselves."

"Jesús stood up and looked out toward the setting sun. 'Not that it will make a difference to them, in the long run. Let's not kid ourselves about where this is going. Look what happened to Juan. In the end the powers that be will get me, too.'

"They all watched a pelican do its awkward dive into the ocean and come back to the surface. The sun was going down now, and the sky was all blue and red and gold. Jesús said, 'It'll be all right. The pelican comes back up again. The sun sets and rises again. They won't find it so easy to get rid of me… It's going to come out all right. It's just the way things have to be, if God is going to rule.' He smiled at the group on the sand. No one smiled back.

"Simon could remember every detail of that scene and every word of Jesús. But he couldn't take it in. None of them could, even though Jesús said the same thing to them again and again. They were in denial. Can you blame them? Could you have accepted it?"

[Could you have accepted it? How well have his followers through the years accepted Jesus' self-definition?]

LOOKING TO THE FUTURE
Luke 9: 23ff.
[journal jottings]

Luke 9:23-24
"Anyone who wishes to follow me must renounce self... Those who give their lives for me will save themselves."

Apparently Jesús was trying to warn his followers: if you're going to follow me, prepare for hard times. Maybe for arrest and execution. But at the same time he was giving them hope: in the long run, when God shows who's running things, you'll be glad you stuck with me. No wonder they had a hard time taking him seriously.

[How thoroughly do you accept Jesus' message of the cross now?]

From here on, my usually reliable source is of less help. I have a number of different stories, sometimes in different versions. They're from different sources, some of them direct, some of them not. Some are about Jesús, some were told by him. Some of them are pretty sketchy and I'll have to try to fill in the details with educated guesses.

THE MARCH ON THE BIG CITY
Luke 9: 28-62
[Notebook insert: pages supposedly from the Informer's diary;
I hope no one ever asks where I got it]

Luke 9:28-62

Jesus took Peter and James and John up the mountain…

When they came down from the mountain…
A man cried out, "Teacher help my son, who has seizures…
I asked your disciples, but they couldn't do anything."
…Jesus healed the boy and gave him back to his father.

After that scene on the beach, we stayed up in the north end of Santa Barbara County for a while. Jesús and a few of his buddies went on a hike up in the hills. They'd do that sometimes. Jesús played favorites.

There was a kid who was really sick – looked like he was having epileptic seizures-- and his father couldn't afford to take him to a doctor. A lot of these people didn't have health insurance. He came looking for Jesús, along with a lot of other people.

I said I'd try to help. I'd seen people do healings, besides Jesús, I mean. I tried lifting up my hands and shouting out, "Be healed! If you have faith, you can be healed!" Shouting didn't seem to help. Some of the others of our group joined me. None of us were very good at this kind of thing. The kid kept moaning and twisting around. Then Jesús showed up. He just said a couple of words and the kid was okay. Jesús acted like we should have done something different. I didn't argue about that. I had bigger worries.

I got Simon and James and John and made them sit down with me. Simon was being very quiet for a change. "What's the matter with you?" I asked him. "You look like you've seen a ghost."

"Not a ghost," he said. "But I've just been told to shut up and listen."

The other two sat there grinning, like they knew something but weren't going to talk about it. I didn't want to talk about them anyway, but about our campaign.

"You've got to help me talk some sense into our man," I said. "I know we're not living in a real democracy, but there's still a way the political game is played, and he's not going about it right. If he wants to be Leader, he's got to have a program that people will respond to. 'Let them kill me and it will turn out all right,' isn't going to sell. He needs a platform--"

"He's got a platform," James interrupted. "Moses gave the people a Constitution to build their national life on, and Jesús is saying let's go back and start over, and re-constitute the nation."

51

While they were on the mountain...

... the appearance of his face and clothes were changed – white and shining. Moses and Elijah appeared, speaking about the "exodus" or passage which he would fulfill in Jerusalem... Jesus told Peter and the others to say nothing about this to anyone.

Luke 9:46
They got into an argument about who was greater among them.
Luke 9:49
"We saw someone casting out demons, and told him to stop."

Luke 9:54
"Should we call down fire from heaven upon them?"

I ignored this burst of unreality. "He needs endorsements," I argued. "Some big names who will line up behind him and support him."

"He's got all the endorsements he needs," John put in.

"Oh yeah? Who?"

"Besides Moses, Elijah."

"Who?!"

"Elijah. The prophet. The one who stood up to the rulers of his own time. The one who had to go underground and spend a good bit of his life on the run. The one who brought about a revolution—"

"Shut up, you guys," said Simon. "You're talking too much." This, from Simon.

"You guys are all nuts," I said. "You're dreaming. Dreams don't make a successful campaign."

After that I didn't try to talk political sense to them any more. I made one last try with Jesús, though.

We were way up in New Cuyama, about as far from civilization as you can imagine. The other guys had been fussing about this and that. They argued with each other about which of them was most important to the program, or project, as if we had one. They got mad when someone used Jesús' name without authorization from them. They were all riled up when people weren't hospitable enough to them. Jesús seemed to think the problem was with their attitudes: they should think of themselves as little children. But these macho types didn't want anyone calling them "Boy."

"The problem," I pointed out, "is that we lack a focus. We're just wandering around, not going anyplace."

"We're going to go some place now," he said. He gathered us around a table in the back of the garage where we'd been meeting. He spread out an old Auto Club map of California. "How far is it from here to Los Angeles?" he asked.

"I don't know," I shrugged. "A couple of hundred miles, as the crow flies?"

"But we're not going to fly there," he told us. "Nor drive. We're going to walk. It'll be the great 1,000-K walk to the big city.

People will join us as we go. By the time we get to L.A. there'll be enough of us to be noticed." And he started tracing a zigzag route from town to town down the coast and inland and back again.

| Luke 9:51 |
| When the time had come for him to be taken up, he set his face toward the road to Jerusalem. |

"We won't get a hundred kilometers, much less a thousand," I warned him. "The Security Force'll stop us in no time."

"The Colonel in Santa Barbara isn't unfriendly. Beyond that, they'll let us go through if we keep moving rather than have the hassle of dealing with us – they'll leave us to the big city cops. And by the time we get near L.A., it'll be Holiday Season, and they'll have other things on their minds."

"So what are we supposed to do when we get there?"

"You remember how Juan said that it was no longer time for business as usual? That's what we'll say. People have got to let God run the show, do things God's way, and the time is now."

"What good will that do? Who's going to pay attention?"

"Sometimes you have to do and say what's right and leave the outcome to God," Jesús said, with a big smile at all of us.

Why would the rest of them go along with this doomed plan? Jesús had a lot of charm, and they would follow him. But it was too late for him to charm me. I want out of this whole crazy enterprise. But how? One can't just walk away and go home, and when the Security Force shows up at the door, say, "Oh, I left the conspiracy before the big riot in L.A. took place." I need to find a way to get free of it, cleanly.

[If you had been with Jesus when "he set his face toward Jerusalem," what would you have said to him? What might you say to him now?]

JESÚS TALKS ABOUT SPIRITUALITY
Luke 10:38-11:13; 18:1-8
[as reported by a friend of Jesús]

**Luke
10: 38-11:13**

**On their journey,
they came to a
town where a
woman named
Martha invited
them to her
home.
Her sister Mary
sat at Jesus' feet
to listen to him…**

At first, Jesús was more Martha's friend than mine. He was important to me, but I never got to talk to him. She was the outgoing one. After her husband died, and I moved in with her, we had a sort of division of effort. She'd go to rallies and marches and meetings. I'd go to the library in my spare time, or to workshops on interior life: Indo-European Rituals, or Ch'an Meditation, or, on one occasion, Quantum Spirituality.

That was what I attended one weekend when Jesús and some of his friends stopped at our house on the way to L.A.. I came back and found Jesús in the living room. Most of "the boys" had gone off shopping for some extra things for supper, and they were taking their time about it. A couple of them were watching TV. Martha, of course, was in the kitchen. I had a chance to talk to Jesús.

I told him about the talk I'd heard on Quantum Spirituality. "So it seems like God is the 'uncaused cause' of quantum effects, including the Big Bang at the Beginning – am I getting all this right? I want to know how to achieve communion with the Source, the Infinite, the All."

He listened attentively, and nodded.

"What about you?" I asked him. "You pray. I know you do. But I've never heard you talk about spirituality. What kind of meditation technique do you use?"

"Maybe," he said, "you're making something complicated out of something that's fairly simple. God is everywhere, in the heavens and on the earth, and is beyond our power to understand or to name, but God is also very close to us, within us. God cares for each of us. I think of God as my Father, and that is how I talk to Him."

"I'd prefer to think of God as Mother, and talk to Her, if I knew how."

"My point is not that God is one gender or another, but that God loves us personally, and speaks to us intimately, and we can speak to God the same way about what's in our hearts."

"And what's in your heart?"

He paused. "I want the world to know God."

**Jesus said,
"When you pray,
say:
'Father,**

**may your name
be made holy;**

may your Kingdom come;

give us each day our daily bread; and forgive us our sins, for we also forgive anyone who owes us anything; and do not let us fall into temptation.'"

"But God is the Unknowable --Mystery – the Other – the Holy."

"Exactly. God is Holy. God is Other. Different. Not like the lords and masters of this world in this age. Not someone you can bribe or manipulate or cajole to do what you want. Not someone you need to bribe or manipulate or cajole to keep from hurting you. God is Love, Justice, Peace. The day is coming when God will show that holiness to the world. I pray for that – the coming of God's Kingdom."

"I've heard you talk about that. I'd prefer the word 'Reign.'"

"All right. The important thing is to want what God wants. To want God's will to be accomplished."

"And what does God want?" I was being a little smart-alecky, but I didn't go so far as to add, "if you know so much."

"Isn't it pretty obvious? For everyone to have what they need to live. For people to get free of the evil that holds them down, to stand firm against the pressures that threaten to overcome their good intentions, to leave behind their hatreds and grudges, to accept God's mercy, and to share in the celebration of God's love."

"Okay," I said, unwilling to let it go. "I've heard you talk before about not being greedy. So you think I should just ask God for what I need, and trust She'll take care of me."

"And what about Martha?"

"What about her? Oh, of course, I meant 'we' and 'us'."

"And who are 'we' and 'us' in that sentence?"

That stopped me for a moment. "It has to be everybody, doesn't it? I can't ask God to give me what I need without hoping that everyone will get what they need. But that won't happen unless – until…"

"When God rules."

"And that's what you hope for?"

"With all my heart and soul and body and mind. That's what I pray for. That's what I long for. That's what I live for. I'd give my life for it. Isn't that what's deepest in your heart?"

Luke 11:13
"Your Father will give the holy spirit to those who ask him."

Luke 18:1-8

Jesus told them a parable about perseverance in prayer. "There was a judge who feared neither God nor any human being. A widow came to him asking for a ruling in her favor. For along time he would not give it to her, but eventually he said to himself, 'Though I fear neither God nor man, I'm going to give this widow her rights, because she keeps bothering me, and in the end she'll beat me up.'
Won't God give justice to his people who cry out day and night?"

Luke 10:42
"Mary has chosen a good role."

I shook my head. "Sure, I want World Peace and Justice for All," I said, wincing at my own clichés, "but I want a few other things closer to home, too. I'm afraid I don't have your spirit."

"Maybe that tells you what you should ask God for."

"I have asked to be a better person, more unselfish, but it doesn't seem to have happened."

Jesús leaned back and gave me a long look. "I've known you and your sister for a while," he said. "Didn't Martha have some trouble with her in-laws after her husband died? Didn't some of them want to get their hands on the house?"

"Yes, and she ran into a judge who could have settled the whole business by signing a little piece of paper, but he wouldn't, 'cause he hoped one party or the other would make it worth his while to favor them."

I smiled as I remembered Martha telling us the story. "She told him she would go to the papers with the story of how corrupt he was.

"He said, 'I'm not afraid of public opinion. This job is a lifetime appointment.'

"She said, 'Some day you'll have to answer to God for this.'

"He said, 'I'm not afraid of God either.'

"She said, 'Then you'd better be afraid of me, buster, 'cause I'm not letting you go.' She didn't threaten him, exactly, but she kept going back and back until he was a little scared, or at least worn out. And she finally got what was hers."

Jesús grinned. "Maybe you could learn something from your sister about perseverance. You think God is more hardhearted than that judge, if you keep asking for the spirit you need?"

"Maybe you could learn something from your sister about hospitality," Martha interrupted at that point. She turned to Jesús. "Tell her to give me a hand. The guys are back with the stuff for supper."

Jesús sighed. "People are always asking me to set someone else straight for them. Martha, we can all help put the food on the table, but what Mary's been talking about is important. The most important thing of all."

After that I noticed he did talk about prayer sometimes in public, but he never said anything different, or very much more, than he said to me that day. And after that he was my friend, too.

[What do you pray for when you pray the Lord's Prayer?
Is it what Jesus prayed for?
What do you want most of all?
Is it what Jesus wanted?]

THE TRAVELER'S STORY
Luke 10:30-37
[insert into notebook]

Luke 10:30-37

A man was going from Jerusalem to Jericho, when he ran into a gang of bandits....

I was on my way to Palm Springs. There was a big convention there of Universal Gnostic Church people interested in new devotional practices. I had left my home in Los Angeles after dark to go down to the desert. About halfway there I noticed I was low on gas. I got off the freeway and found a gas station, one of those small independent stations where a kid is sitting in a booth behind the pumps and you serve yourself.

I was standing by the pump when the kid comes running out of the booth and goes tearing past me. Right behind him are two guys with pistols. They must have been trying to rob the place, but when they saw me, they quit chasing the kid and hit me upside the head with their pistols, one, two, and a couple more whacks as I fell down. Then they kicked me a few times when I was on the ground. Then they grabbed by wallet and my watch and my car keys and took off in my car. The kid who'd been in the booth never came back.

They left him half dead...

I tried to crawl over to the booth where I thought there might be a phone, but I was too weak to make it. I just lay there bleeding near the door.

A priest went by but ignored him...

After a while another car came into the station and drove up to the pump. When the driver got out, I saw he was a minister – wearing a clergyman's uniform. I tried to call to him, but my voice was pretty weak. Maybe he thought I was drunk, or trying to trick him. Anyway he didn't respond. He just filled up his tank and drove off.

Also a Levite...

More time passed and another car drove up. This time I even recognized the driver as a deacon from my own church. He must have been going to the same convention I was. I called out to him. But he didn't recognize me. Well, I was a mess. He just said, "Sorry, buddy, I'm late for a meeting," and drove away.

I thought I was just going to lie there and die. But finally a third driver arrived. This one was a woman. She came over and took a good look at me and said, "Man, you sure are in trouble. We better get you some help."

Finally someone showed up who felt compassion for him and bandaged his wounds and took him to an inn, and told the innkeeper, 'I'll pay the bill on my way back'

She got me into her car, somehow, and drove to an emergency clinic – it was quite a ways away. She waited while they put some stitches in me and bandaged me up. Then she took me to a motel and used her own credit card to get a room for me. "You better call the cops and tell them what happened," she said. "Me, I've got to get on to

The compassionate stranger was a Samaritan.

Go and do likewise.

where I was going. I'll come back in the morning and see how you're doing."

And she did. She even gave me a ride back to Los Angeles. Eventually the cops found my car and insurance paid for most of what the carjackers had done to it. But I wasn't able to pay that woman back, because she never did tell me her name or address.

Now what I forgot to mention is that this woman was black. And you know that means she probably wasn't a member of the UGC – more likely one of those independent churches where they do a lot of shouting and waving their arms. But she was the one who helped me out, not my own church folks. So I was pretty sour on my own church, but I couldn't see myself hollering and swaying in church like some of them do. So I wasn't sure where I belonged.

Eventually I met Jesús, and that gave me a new direction for my life. I even told him this story. He loved it. He helped me understand what it meant. I ended up feeling a little ashamed of myself for caring too much about races and devotional styles, instead of what God cares about.

[Whom have you gone out of your way to help, directly or indirectly? In our contemporary globalized world, how can we apply this story?]

59

THE DUTIFUL DAUGHTER'S STORY
Luke 15:11-32
[notebook insert]

Luke 15:11-32

A man had two sons, and the younger said to his father, "Give me my share of the family's money." Shortly after, the son left... After he has spent all the money, he was destitute... Eventually he returned home and was welcomed by his faither.

The older son was out in the fields, ans when he came toward the house, he heard music... "Your brother is home..." The older son was angry and would not go into the house. His father came out and tried to reason with him. "We have to celebrate and rejoice: your brother was dead, and lives; he was lost, and has been found."

I was just twenty and my sister was eighteen when she left. She just took off one day, with the family car, my mother's credit card, and a goofy boyfriend. They went to San Francisco; he dumped her; she took up with someone else, and then someone else; the credit card was maxed out, the car broke down, and she ended up flipping burgers and going hungry after she paid her rent. We found all this out later. For a couple of years we just didn't hear from her, and I myself didn't want to hear of her ever again. Her taking off meant I was left to try to finish college while holding two jobs and helping mom with our rent and the care of the little kids.

One day I get home from work and as soon as I park in the driveway I can tell something's going on. My little brother runs out and says, "Guess what? Our sister's home!"

I go to the front door and see a bunch of people I don't know in the living room and dining room and there on the couch is my sister, with my mom next to her, hugging her and laughing. I turn around and slam the door behind me and go back and get in the car and just sit there, fuming. My mom comes out and gets in the car on the passenger side and puts her hand on my arm and says, "Come on inside. What's the matter with you?"

And I go, "Your favorite daughter shows up after all this time and you throw a big party for her. When's the last time you did that for me?" And I know how childish it sounds but that's the way I feel.

My mom goes, "We had to have a party. Your sister was lost, and now we've found her again. She was as good as dead, and we have her back alive." And she starts crying. I couldn't stand it.

So I get out of the car again and slam the door behind me and go in the house and slam that door too and there in front of me is Jesús. I could have sunk into a crack in the floor and vanished. I mean, I wished I could have. But my mom makes me say hello to my sister and sit down on the couch between her and Jesús. It turns out he and his crowd had been going through town on the way to L.A. and my mom invited him to eat at our place. And then my sister showed up.

My mom brings us plates full of the roast veal she's cooked up for the occasion. I don't feel like eating anything. Jesús says to me, "What's wrong?" And I end up telling him how I feel: angry and ashamed of myself and frustrated because I don't understand myself let alone being able to say anything to my sister.

Jesús taps his glass with his spoon until he's got everyone's attention. He says, "Some of you have joined me on this walk just recently, and before that, you were living lives you're not so proud of now. Others have been with me a long time, and maybe you resent these newcomers. I think these young women have something to say to us."

So my sister tells her story and I tell my story and then we're both crying and my mom is crying and we're all hugging each other and some of Jesús' people are looking relieved and others are looking embarrassed and a couple are looking like a light bulb just turned on in their heads.

Jesús says to me, "You mind if I tell this story to other folks who might need to hear it?" And I go, "No." And I guess he did tell it, after, to other people who figured they deserved something extra because they'd been so good.

[Could you play the part of any of the characters in this story?
If you did, what would Jesus say to you?
What would you say to him?]

THE BUSINESSMAN'S STORY
Luke 16:1-13
[insert into notebook]

That year, I was the program chairman for the monthly meeting of our businessmen's, excuse me, business persons', luncheon club. And that month, just before Holiday Season, our guest speaker cancelled on us. Now, I had heard that Jesús was passing through town, on his way to L.A., and I knew someone who knew someone who was able to contact him with an invitation. He accepted.

As dessert was being served, I introduced him as our substitute guest speaker and thanked him for coming on short notice. He got up to speak and gave a short, forceful talk about the way the world would be if we let God rule, and how the time was coming when God would reign over us, and how we needed to get ready now for that day. He hinted that some of us might join him on his walk to the city, though I didn't expect any of us would really want to wear out an expensive pair of shoes that way.

I thought he deserved more attention than my colleagues were giving him. Some were stirring their coffee, clinking spoons and saucers, some were conducting whispered business among themselves, a couple went outside to smoke. I found myself thinking that what he was saying was important, and I needed to give it serious thought, but when? I started scrolling through my Palm Pilot and realizing that I didn't have a free day, or free evening, for weeks, maybe months to come. Perhaps, I thought, in a year or two, my business will have reached the point where I can take time to think about God and the world.

Then I realized Jesús was looking at me. "I'll conclude my remarks with an anecdote taken from real life," he said.

"There was a certain dealer in financial instruments and commodities futures whose career took him to be Vice President of his brokerage company. He was clever, but not too honest. One day, a Thursday, he realized that the CEO of the company suspected him of embezzling company funds. He didn't think they could get enough on him to have him arrested, but he knew he'd be fired.

"That night he had nightmares, imagining himself standing on a street corner amid a crowd of day laborers trying to get work – but no one would hire him, because he looked too scrawny. Then he saw himself as a panhandler in an alley someplace. He woke up in a cold sweat and spent the rest of the night figuring out what to do.

Luke 16:1-13

There was a rich man who had a steward who was accused of mismanaging his money...

"Turn in your accounts; you're fired."

"I can not dig; I'm ashamed to beg. I know what I will do, so that others will take me in when I lose this position."

> He called in those who owed his master money, and told each, "Rewrite the bill for a smaller amount."
>
> The master praised the steward's cleverness.
>
> The children of this age are wiser than the children of light in their own business.
>
> You cannot serve God and Mammon.... If you're not trustworthy in money matters, who will entrust you with more important things?... Make friends for yourself with your dirty money, so that they may receive you into eternal dwellings.

"Next morning he went to work and put his plan into action. He'd always been tough in dealing with his counterparts in other firms, when they were in a weaker position. Now he called them up, one after another, and said, 'You're a valuable trading partner and we haven't always shown our appreciation. Now, let's renegotiate that last contract.' At 5:00 p.m. he handed in a letter of resignation. Then he went on vacation. His last day's dealings had cost his firm a lot of money, and he figured his CEO would be furious. But he also figured that when he returned, he'd have friends in other companies who'd help him get a job.

"The CEO's reaction was: 'If he wants to work someplace else, I'll even write him a letter of recommendation: He's a crook, but he's a smart crook.'

"Now, you are smart business people, and some of you have made fast deals when you had to. Why is it that people can move fast when their financial interests are at stake, but are so slow when their eternal destiny is at stake?"

He looked at me again and sat down.

Afterwards, I heard some of my colleagues discussing it. "My rabbi gave a talk like that once," said one. "He said we shouldn't let money rule our lives. It's hard to care about success and not make it our god. He's got a point."

"I think his point," another objected, "was that we shouldn't be making crooked deals, because if we can't be trusted in business dealings, God won't bless us with spiritual riches."

"No," said another, "he wants us to give our money to charity, or to the poor. Make friends with the poor. They're the ones he says will be the important people when God's Kingdom comes."

I was sure I knew what he meant when he looked at me. The time to decide is now, it's a critical moment, don't miss it.

I do need to stop and think about all this and decide what I'm going to do about it. And I will. Eventually.

[Consider the various morals to the story – about good use of money, about taking action while there's time – suggested by Luke's Gospel. Do any of them apply to you?]

THE LOAN SHARK
Luke 19:1-10
[insert into notebook]

Luke 19:1-10

On his journey, Jesus was going through Jericho. There was a man named Zacchaeus, a leader among the tax collectors, and rich. He wanted to see Jesus, but he couldn't, because he was short, and there was a big crowd. So he climbed a sycamore tree along Jesus' route. Jesus, seeing him, said, "Zacchaeus, come down quickly! Today I am coming to your house." "I give half of my goods to the poor, and if I have cheated anyone, I make fourfold restitution!"

I considered myself a legitimate businessman. My neighbors called me a loan shark and a snitch for the IRS. But I never broke anyone's kneecaps, nor threatened to, and though the government was a lousy government they still needed tax money, I figured. Still, the truth is, I was fed up with the life I was living. I was tired of having my neighbors look down on me, figuratively as well as literally. But what was I going to do? A person has to make a living.

In those days I operated out of a small house in Venice. The neighborhood then wasn't as expensive as it is now. I heard that Jesús was going to lead his marchers through the area. It was out of his way, going from up the coast to downtown L.A., but I guess he wasn't in a hurry. I wanted to see him. Somehow I thought that might make a difference in my life.

This particular day I hear a lot of noise outside and I realize the march must be coming through my neighborhood. I went outside to look. It turned out they were coming right down my street. But the street is narrow, and full of people, and I'm a little guy, and my neighbors are not going to make room for me to see anything. So I climb up on top of my SUV which is parked right in front of my house.

Jesús comes down the street and looks up at me and points at me and shouts, "You! Zack! I'm having supper at your place tonight!" My neighbors all glare at me and some of them even start booing. My head is spinning; I'm dizzy; my whole life flashes before my eyes, and I don't like what I see.

I look around at my neighbors. "Have I ever cheated any of you?" I yell. 'I'll pay you back with interest! Double! Triple! No, make that quadruple!" I was on a roll. "You think I make money off the poor people of this neighborhood? Okay, I'll clean out my bank account and give it to the local food pantry! And the thrift shop!" Even in my condition then, I was thinking to myself, "Of course, I mean my checking account, not my savings account."

Jesus said: "Today salvation has come to this house, for this man also is a son of Abraham."

Jesús looked around at everyone as if to say, "You see? He's really one of us, after all, isn't he?"

The local paper printed a picture of me standing up on top of the car waving my arms. They wanted to show how foolish I looked, how foolish all of Jesús' followers were. Eventually, all of the copies of that edition were confiscated. But I managed to save the picture. It was about all I managed to save from that time. I don't care if I looked foolish. I'm proud of it.

[Who are the least forgivable offenders in our society? How would Jesus deal with them? How would you like to deal with them?]

Luke 19:28-42

When they reached the outskirts of Jerusalem, Jesus sent two disciples into town.

He said, "You'll find a donkey on which no one has ridden... Tell anyone who asks, 'The master needs it.'"...

They brought it to Jesus...

As he rode along, people threw their garments on the road in front of him.

THE OWNER OF THE PICKUP TRUCK
Luke 19:28-40
[insert into notebook]

The Security Force called us "urban cells of subversion". That made us sound a lot more organized than we were. There were just a few of us in the city who knew a few people who knew Jesús, that's all. In my case, it was a cousin of mine, who was marching with Jesús.

It was Holiday Season. I was going to relax in my little bungalow in the Crenshaw District, and watch the Holiday Season Parade on TV, instead of going up to Wilshire Boulevard to watch it. This was in the old days, before the Great Riots, or the Uprising, or whatever you want to call it, back when you could have a parade down Wilshire. Quite a thing it was, from Westwood to downtown.

I was watching the beginning of it: Archbishop Hannan gave a blessing in the name of the Universal Gnostic Church. Then a squad of Security Force troops led off the parade, brandishing their latest gadgets, with a platoon of armored vehicles behind them and an overflight by helicopters. They were trying to impress us with how crazy it would be to try any trouble-making during the Holidays. They certainly impressed me. Then came the big corporate advertising floats. Really big.

Then I glanced out the window and saw what looked like some fool trying to steal my new pick-up truck. I ran outside and saw it was my cousin. "We need a truck," he said. "*He* needs *your* truck."

"Well, you just had to ask," I told him, and got behind the wheel. "Where to?"

We didn't have to go a long way, just to the corner of Wilshire and Westwood, the beginning of the parade route. Jesús was waiting there, with a whole crowd of people around him and behind him. We got there just as the last of the official parade vehicles, a gussied-up taxicab, was starting down Wilshire. Jesús smiled and waved at me and climbed up onto the bed of the truck. My cousin said, "Follow that cab."

We drove, slowly of course, down the boulevard, and the crowds around us kept shouting to the crowds in front of us, "Jesús is coming!" After a while the word got ahead of us and people along the way were shouting, "Jesús! Jesús! Yeah! Yeah!" Jesús was smiling

As they went down the road toward the city, the crowds were shouting, "Blessed the king who comes in the name of the Lord! Peace in heaven, glory in the highest!" Some of the religious leaders said, "Teacher, reproach your disciples." He answered, "If they were silent, the stones would cry out."

"They will not leave one stone upon another stone."

and waving at people all along the way. Somebody got the idea of taking off his jacket and waving it, and then that caught on, and lots of people were waving their jackets and sweaters and some were throwing them in the air and some were throwing them into the street. The security people – not SecForce troops, just temporary security agency guards – didn't know what to do.

We came to where we had to pass the reviewing stand. The parade officials had been about to leave but they stopped when they heard the shouting and saw the waving. When we got in front of them someone got on the P.A. system and shouted, "Stop this disturbance!" He was looking at Jesús. "You're responsible for this! Stop it!"

Just at that moment a gap opened in the crowd and you could see where someone had written graffiti on the wall of a building: "The people united will never be defeated! *Arriba el pueblo! Abajo el gobierno!*" Jesús shouted back at the reviewing stand, "That's what you get when you try to silence everyone!"

We managed to get to the end of the parade route without getting shot at or trampled by the crowds. Jesús got down from the back of the truck, thanked me for its use, and started walking through downtown.

His followers were gawking around at the big buildings, the banks, the government offices, the cultural center, the cathedral, like a bunch of country kids who'd never been to town before. The last thing I heard Jesús say was, "Don't be too impressed. All this stuff is going to come down. Every brick of it." And that was way before the Great Riots, or Uprising, or whatever you want to call it.

I was scared, I'll admit. I'd never been in any scene like that. And I never had a day like that since.

My old pick-up is still in the garage. I hardly drove it after that. Couldn't bring myself to risk denting it. I take real good care of it. That must be the most pampered pick-up truck in the world.

[In this imaginary scene, people are taking risks: Jesús, the driver, the cheering crowds. In real life, what risks have you taken? What would you be willing to risk for Jesus?]

THE TOURIST'S STORY
Luke 19:45-46
[insert into notebook]

Luke 19:45-46

Martha and I had planned for a long time to take this tour of Los Angeles during the Holiday Season. We found good companions on the bus with us. Some, like Martha, were more religious types; I found some fellow thinkers, teachers from the English Department of our community college, to talk with. Someone had heard that the man they called Jesús was going to be in the city during the Holidays. Martha and her friends were excited: they wanted to see him do a miracle. I was mildly interested; I'd heard he was a good speaker and a bit of a philosopher, and thought I might like to hear him.

When we got to downtown L.A., our bus was met by a nice young man who greeted us, "Hello, my name is Saul. I'll be your guide today." But he let us know quickly enough that he wasn't going to be a guide all his life; he really was a writer. I guess a lot of people are like that in L.A. Martha was impressed because he said he was going to write about religious tradition.

He started leading us down this big avenue, pointing out the big bank buildings, the government buildings, and the cathedral, toward which we were heading. It was hard to stick together with our group. The streets were filled with people, more than the usual crowds, according to Saul. A lot of them didn't look like city people, more like folks who'd come in from the country.

Just as we got to the cathedral plaza we heard a lot of noise and confusion up ahead of us. It looked like someone was kicking over the tables in the cathedral gift shop. And someone had trashed the ATM machine near it. A man came out into the plaza, followed by a dozen or so others, chanting, "Shut it down! Shut it down!"

Someone else was yelling, "Security! Security!" and some men in uniforms came running into the plaza and confronted the man who seemed to be the leader of the demonstrators. They're face to face, practically shouting at each other. I couldn't hear everything they were saying, but the guard wanted to know if the demonstrators had a permit, though of course they couldn't. The leader of the mob said something about this place becoming like a gangsters' compound. And it sounded like he was threatening to tear it down.

I told Martha, "This is not just a riot, it's becoming a revolution. It's time for us to get out of here." Saul lead us, half running, half walking, back to our bus. All along the avenue, people

[Note: Mark and John give longer accounts of this scene. In its final version, Luke's Gospel summarizes it in these few words:]

Entering the Temple, Jesus began to throw out the merchants, telling them, "It is written, 'My house shall be a house of prayer,' but you have made it 'a robbers' den.'"

were crowding around the banks and the government buildings, shouting, "Shut it down! Shut it down!"

When we were safe again on the bus, Saul said, "I'm sorry, folks, but we couldn't foresee that incident. As you might have guessed, that was the man they call Jesús."

One of my new buddies asked, "Are you sure? I thought he was supposed to be a smart man. That display looked pretty foolish to me."

Martha said, "I thought he was supposed to be a great miracle worker. That was pathetic."

Saul repeated, "I'm sorry about this. I don't think the tour company can give you a refund, but I'll try to see that you get vouchers for a future trip."

Right, as my kids would say, like we're going to do something like this again.

But as a matter of fact, years later, we did take another tour, this time to San Diego, and when we got there we were going through a park and saw a man giving a speech to a small crowd of listeners, and Martha said, "Look! That's the young man who met us in Los Angeles that day!" And I couldn't stop her from going up and asking him, "Aren't you Saul? I thought you were going to be a writer."

"Not any more," he told us. "I'm known as Paul now. Everything I used to think was so important seems like a lot of trash to me since I came to know Jesús."

"But he was executed!" I reminded him.

"Exactly," said Saul/Paul. "Consecrated and sent by God, to bring the power and wisdom of God to us."

"I thought he looked pretty foolish," I said.

"I thought he was pathetic," Martha reminded us.

"God's foolishness," said Paul, "is wiser than human wisdom, and God's weakness is stronger than human power."

A lot of nonsense, I still say. If he wanted to change the world, he should have had better strategy. If he wanted to start a revolution, he should have learned about guerilla tactics. We Americans don't necessarily need to see signs and wonders, we can forgive someone

---

I Corinthians 1:22-25

The Jews – traditional religious people – look for signs, miracles; the Greeks – who think of themselves as up to date intellectuals – look for wisdom, that is, cleverness; but we proclaim Christ crucified – to the Jews, a shocking scandal, to the Greeks, foolishness, but to God's chosen ones, whether from Jewish or Greek backgrounds, the power of God and the wisdom of God; for the foolishness of God is wiser than human wisdom, and the weakness of God is more powerful than human strength."

who doesn't talk like an intellectual, but we do demand results. If Jesús' way had been effective, it might have been a different story.

[Does it sometimes seem to you that God is weak and/or unaware of what's going on? Does Jesus' way of non-violent action – and acceptance of suffering – seem right to you?]

THE CAMERAMAN
Luke 20
[insert into notebook]

The boss figured that Jesús would come back downtown and told us – the news crew – to hang around and get an interview with him. The boss was right, but not alone: every other news crew in town had the same orders. So when Jesús showed up on the steps of the cathedral, there was a whole crowd of reporters sticking microphones in his face and asking him questions.

I've been shooting news events a long time. I don't kid myself about objective reporting. But what they were doing at this scene was pretty heavy-handed. It was too obvious. The lords of the media had ordered the news editors to get something on Jesús, and the reporters were doing their best.

Right away they were in his face about the fuss he'd been causing. "Did you get a permit for that parade down Wilshire? Who authorized that rally, or whatever it was, at the cathedral?"

I thought Jesús was a small-town boy who'd get swallowed alive in the big city, but he kept his cool pretty well. He looked at the reporters and said, "I'll answer that if you tell me who authorized John to do what he did."

Well, no one wanted to handle that hot potato. Say that John was sent by God and you'd be in trouble with the authorities; say he wasn't, and you'd lose ratings with the public. So they changed the subject.

Someone threw a curve at him. "What about the people who say the Harriman administration is anti-religious and we shouldn't support them with our money? Don't you think religious people should support tax resisters?"

Jesús put his hands in his pockets and then held them up, empty. "I don't seem to have any money with me. Anyone got a bill?" The reporter who'd asked the question fished in her purse and pulled out a twenty.

Jesús asked her, "Whose picture is on it?"

She said, "Harriman Senior's, of course."

He said, "It looks like you're the one who's carrying that man's money. If he wants it back, maybe you should give it back to him. But

---

Luke 20:1-10

They asked, "By what authority are you doing the things you do?" He answered, "You tell me: was the baptism of John from heaven, or from human authority?" They said, "We don't know."

Luke 20:20-26
Those who were watching him sent conspirators to ask, "Is it right to pay tribute to Caesar?" Jesus said, "Show me the coin. Whose image and inscription does it bear?" "Caesar's." …"Give back to Caesar what belongs to Caesar; …

71

and to God, what belongs to God."

Luke 20:27-40

Certain religious liberals asked him: "Teacher, there were seven brothers, and each in turn married the same woman and died. At the 'Resurrection' whom will she belong to?" Jesus said, "In this age, there are marriages and marriage customs; it will be different in the age to come... God is the God of the living."

don't forget whose image you bear, and don't give Harriman what belongs to God."

No one knew what to make of that. The only sure thing was that they hadn't made him look bad.

Someone else stuck a microphone in his face. He tried to make it sound like a friendly question, but you could tell what he thought about old-fashioned religious ideas. "Do you really uphold traditional religious values and beliefs? You've heard about – (he mentioned some movie star, I honestly don't remember his name) – just got married for the seventh time? Well, if the dead are going to rise again, does he have seven wives for all eternity? Is that your idea of heaven?"

Jesús said, "Is it your idea that a man owns his wife? That he can just discard her whenever he wants? Is it your idea that things will always be the way they are now? In the new world that is coming, things are going to be different. When the dead rise again, we'll all find out what it's like to be children of God. Meanwhile, we know God gives us life. And God will always give us life."

There were some other questions, but it was the same kind of stuff. They kept going after him from the right and from the left, but they couldn't stop him. He'd keep turning the tables on them, answer their questions with questions of his own, even ask them to give interpretations of Scripture passages, which of course they couldn't do. I wanted to applaud, but I didn't want to lose my grip on the camera, and I couldn't afford to lose my job. It was clear that no matter what he said, they were after him, and they were going to get him.

[If you were able to address a question to Jesus in public, what would you ask him? Do you sometimes find his words hard to understand? Do you trust that his teachings are right, and worth trying to understand?]

FINAL ENTRIES IN THE INFORMER'S DIARY
Luke 22:1-53
[insert in notebook]

Luke 22:1-53

As the Passover approached, the religious leaders were looking for a way to eliminate Jesus, but they feared the popular reaction. … Judas Iscariot went and talked to them and made an agreement to betray him in return for money…

When the Passover came, Jesus sent Peter and John to prepare the Passover dinner. "Look for a man carrying a water jar, and follow him…"

An argument broke out over who should be greater.

I have found a way out of the mess Jesús has got me into. Obviously they would like to arrest him and obviously they are afraid to do so with crowds all around during the Holiday Season. And they don't know where he and the rest of us are, at night, when we're not in the public eye. But I do. It's clever, hiding in plain sight. Anyone on the roof of Pilato's headquarters with a night vision 'scope could see us easily, if they knew where to look. And we've got a good view of central Los Angeles from our campsite on a hillside just east of downtown. There's not much else to recommend it. The site is too steep for even the greediest developer to do anything with it. Clinging to it are a few scraggly palms and olive trees – and us.

So how am I going to take advantage of my inside information? I'm not going near Security Force or Fourth Division Headquarters. But the Universal Gnostic Church has its own private security guards, and contacts with the police too. I hope they don't shuffle me off to some pompous clerical bureaucrat who won't be bothered to do anything.

…. … …. ….   … ….

It wasn't as bad as I feared. The receptionist at the UGC main office let me talk to a secretary, who passed me on to … well, eventually I found myself in the office of someone with enough authority to make my trip there worthwhile. He was quite reasonable. Understood exactly what I was suggesting. Offered to "reimburse me for expenses" with very little hinting on my part. When we'd made the deal, he took me to another part of the building and introduced me to the head of their private security guards. That gentleman gave me a phone number with which I can reach him at any hour. The rest should be easy.

… … … … … … …

It was easy and it wasn't. Our Holiday Season dinner was a disaster. If I had known where it was going to be, I could have made my move beforehand, but it was set up in a very hush-hush way: some of our group sent down to Sunset Boulevard to spot a man doing last-minute shopping and follow him home and get things set up and then lead the rest of us there. Jesús was being pretty careful.

At dinner Peter and the others got into an argument about who would have the most power in the Kingdom. What Kingdom?! Jesús kept talking about serving the rest of us, giving his life for us, pouring out his blood, giving his body for us. He let out a hint that he suspected what I was about. I couldn't follow everything that was going on. Eventually I couldn't take it any more and gave some excuse and went out.

Needless to say, I didn't go back. I used the cell phone the security agency head had given me to call him and set up a meeting place. I wasn't simply going to tell him where to pick up Jesús after dinner – if I were going to collect for my "expenses," I had to be there.

It was after dark when we had our rendezvous. I was upset to find that he had brought not only his own employees but the police SWAT team and even observers from Fourth Division HQ. I insisted that we go in quietly, just myself and a few of them, while the rest of the troops manned the perimeter at some distance. "You won't be able to recognize him in the dark, anyway," I pointed out. "I will. I'll go up and give him a big *abrazo*. Then you can close in and grab him. The rest don't matter. They're just sheep. It's the shepherd you want."

When I was sure that Jesús and his friends had had enough time to get there, I led the way to our camping spot, going down from the top of the hill. It took me a few minutes to spot Jesús. He was lying face down on the ground, and I thought he was asleep. Then I saw that his shoulders were shaking. After all his brave talk, he was crying! For myself, I would like death with dignity.

He stood up, and even by moonlight I could see that his forehead was covered with sweat. Or was it blood? But his face was calm now.

He went down the hill a way and woke up a couple of the others. I followed and when I was close enough I could see that his expression was not only calm but determined – like someone who's been agonizing over a tough decision but has made up his mind. That almost stopped me in my tracks. But there was no way I could stop now. The police were right on my heels. I went up and hugged Jesús like a long lost friend and he said, "So that's how you do it?" He didn't flinch. He didn't back down from the police, either. "You come to arrest me as if I were a gangster," he said. "But it seems that you're the ones who have to act under cover of darkness."

Out of the corner of my eye I saw one of the gang pull a knife and take a swing at one of the security guards. I couldn't believe the stupidity of it. Then the helicopter came down and pinned us in its spotlight and the dogs started barking and the police and soldiers rushed in from the perimeter and the rest of Jesús' loyal buddies ran off in every direction.

… … … … …

It's been days now, weeks even. Sometimes I go and check out the places where we used to hang out, like the house where we had that final dinner. Sometimes I can tell that the others are still meeting there, and when I get close enough, sometimes I hear them talking and its obvious they're eating and drinking together. And singing and laughing. Don't they know how to grieve? Are they in some kind of deep denial?

I suppose I could drop a dime, as they say on TV, on the whole bunch together. But what would be the point? I've got my immunity. I've got my reward money. I have no reason to do anything. I have no reason to do anything at all.

[Are there moments in your life of which you are ashamed? Or about which you think with embarrassment? Do you trust in the Lord's forgiveness of...whatever?}

THE ADJUTANT'S STORY
Luke 23:1-56
[insert into notebook]

<table>
<tr>
<td>

Luke 23:1-56

After they had taken him to the high priest's house, where he was beaten and interrogated, they brought him to Pilate.

</td>
<td>

It was Holiday Season. I had been hoping the day would be quiet and the General would go home early and let me take the rest of the day off. As long as he was in his office, I had to stay with him, partly to carry out any errand he might think of, partly to be witness to his cleverness.

This day began quietly. He shuffled through papers at his desk. I stood by. Then there was a knock at the office door and when I opened it the duty officer said, "I thought I'd better tell the General personally. They've arrested Jesús."

The General heard it. His eyes narrowed, as they did when he was not happy. "Who arrested him? Not our troops?"

"No," said the officer. "Some private security agency nabbed him."

The General's eyes narrowed further. "What private security agency?"

"They work for the Universal Gnostic Church. But they turned him over to the local cops and they've brought him here. He's in the holding tank down in the basement right now."

"Nobody wants responsibility for taking care of the popular hero…?" The General got up and walked over to the window and looked down at the street, twelve stories below. "What's going on down there?"

The officer didn't know. He got on his phone and called the man stationed at the door. After a quick interchange he reported, "There's some kind of demonstration going on. It seems a bit confused. Some of the crowd are chanting 'Free Jesús!' and others are calling for Hidalgo." He listened again and said, "That Bishop who calls himself Califas is there."

"That phony? What's he want? Maybe I'll ask him. No, wait. Send up this Jesús character first."

The General looked at me. "You're thinking that I should just have the troops break up that crowd down below." I hadn't been thinking that, but he had. He had ordered troops to fire into crowds of civilians before, and he'd do it again. "But I don't want a massacre during Holiday Season."

</td>
</tr>
</table>

So they brought up Jesús, who looked, as most people who'd been in that basement did, in sad shape: bruises on his face, one eye swollen shut, bleeding from cuts on his head.

"So you're the Liberator they talk about, the new Leader of the People?"

I had to give Jesús credit: he held his head up and looked the General in the eye. "That's your language, not mine." But he didn't deny it. In fact, he didn't say anything more.

The General sent him back to the cell in the basement. I opened the door for him and his guards and led the way to the elevator. As they were getting on it, I said to Jesús, "I don't have any sympathy for people like you, but you were stupid not to be a little more cooperative in there. You might have got off the hook. The General isn't looking for trouble during the Holiday Season."

"You have no idea," he said, "how much I wanted to avoid this whole scene. How much I agonized over it. But I'm not backing out now."

The elevator doors closed. I went back to the General.

"Let the good Bishop in," he said. "But not up here. I'll see him down in the lobby."

We went down together to the ground floor and found that the guards had let in Bishop Califas, plus a few others. "We need to let you know," said the Bishop, "that there are many people who are deeply concerned about this issue."

"You mean Jesús? What exactly do we have on him, anyway?"

"He's a subversive," said Califas, as if that were all that needed to be said. And ordinarily it would have been. But not during Holiday Season.

"You mean he made a racket at your cathedral the other day. Why should I care about your religious problems?"

"Not just religious. Marx said, 'The critique of religion is the foundation of all social criticism.'"

"I know what Marx said. And I know he was quoting someone else," the General replied, demonstrating his cleverness. "But I'm not going to do your dirty work at the cost of provoking a riot."

"The man has supported tax resistance. He has advocated violent revolution. That demonstration threatened the whole economic and political core of the city."

Again, I read the General's expression. He had his own sources and knew Jesus' real positions better than Califas thought he did. And he didn't like getting political advice from someone like the Bishop. He might go against it just to spite Califas. On the other hand, he was aware of the tight ties between the Universal Gnostic Church and the business leaders, the real movers and shakers of the city, and their friends in Washington.

Hearing that he was from Galilee, Pilate sent him to Herod, who was visiting Jerusalem. Herod mocked him and sent him back.

Just then the duty officer interrupted. "It's Governor Herrold on the line," he said. "He's staying in town, over at the Bonaventure. He wants to talk to you about Jesús." The General's expression said, "How many idiots do I have to put up with in one day?" Bishop Califas, pushing his luck, pointed out, "Jesús could be considered under the Governor's jurisdiction. He did some of his agitation up north."

The General had the Bishop wait while he returned to his office to take the Governor's call. As we went up he said to me, "Perhaps I can work something out with Herrold. I don't like him, and he doesn't like me, but he has contacts in Washington, and it wouldn't hurt to have a better relationship with him. If he wants to deal with this, maybe I'll let him. Let people be mad at him." He wanted me to admire his strategy and tactics.

And Herod and Pilate, who had been enemies, became friends...

As a tactic, it wasn't effective. Herrold, always a lightweight, was not serious about dealing with Jesús, just curious. But as a strategy, it worked: the General and the Governor became political allies in time.

So we were back to the lobby and the Bishop and his crowd.

Pilate said, "I will punish him and let him go."

The General said, "I'm just letting you know, as a courtesy. Pending more and better evidence against Jesús, I'm having him held by the Security Force. I'm sure they will be as considerate of him as they are of other prisoners." That, he meant, should give you some satisfaction: the man you hate will be hurting a lot. When he's released, if he's released, he'll have learned a lesson.

They said, "Not him! Let Barabbas go!"

Califas and his crew were not happy. They pushed their luck some more. "What about letting Hidalgo go?"

"Hidalgo?" the General said, as if he'd never heard of the thug. "Odd name."

"It's Spanish, from *hijo de alguno*, son of someone, that is, someone from an important family. Unfortunately our poor Hidalgo had neither father nor good family upbringing. You know how it is with these kids. They get into the wrong company, and that leads to bad behavior, and sometimes they justify it with political rhetoric. But this is not a bad boy. Release him into my custody and I guarantee his good behavior in the future. Meanwhile, some of the same people who call Jesús the 'Liberator' are supporters of freedom for Hidalgo. So you can calm them down and give yourself an opening to deal with the real troublemaker."

The demonstration outside was getting noisier. It was getting to the point where something would have to give, or some people were going to get killed.

Pilate finally gave them what they asked for.

The General shrugged. "I'll accept your offer to take custody of this Hidalgo," he said. I knew he was thinking, "And you'll pay for this in time to come."

Eventually I saw what happened to Jesús on a videotape. It got back to headquarters before it was destroyed, and it shows Security Force personnel at work.

They took Simon the Cyrenean and made him carry the cross, after Jesus. Some women and other people followed him, weeping…

They took Jesús from our headquarters in an unmarked car. By that time the only people left from the morning's demonstration were a few women, weeping and wailing on our doorstep. But they saw him being taken away and followed in their own cars. This procession wound its way up into the San Gabriel Mountains. (An odd detail: the SecForce car had a flat tire and they drafted a passerby to help change it. Our men were too embarrassed to report that.) They pulled off the road in an area full of pine trees. They must have known that the women had followed, and even that one of them had brought a camcorder – a gutsy move! – but they were SecForce, so what did they care?

They came to a place called Calvary, and there they crucified him, with a bandit on his right and on his left.

The videotape showed three men being hauled out of the car. It must have been general clean-up time for subversives and bandidos. There was no sound on the tape, and the picture was grainy, but you could make out what was going on. They cuffed the three men to three trees, side by side. Their arms were fastened to tree limbs above their heads. If left alone, they would have died a slow death by suffocation when they got too tired to stand.

But they weren't just left there. The SecForce men took out their pistols and started shooting, slowly, one after another, taking target practice at the bodies of the men on the trees. First a bullet through an arm, then one through a foot.

*[Note: In fact,
Pilate was
recalled to Rome
eventually, and
vanished from
history. Annas
and Caiaphas did
continue to
persecute the
followers of
Jesus.]*

*[Luke's is the
Gospel that gives
us these words.]*

Watching the tape, I could see one of the men was looking at Jesús and yelling, probably cursing. The other said something, too; I couldn't tell what, but he looked very different. Then Jesús looked at him and said something. And – I couldn't believe it – the man smiled. Jesús looked out at the shooters and said something else, either to them or about them. Then one of them put a shot right through his heart.

The light went out of the picture at that point. As I recall, there was a big storm that day, unusual weather for the Season. Evidently the sky got very dark up there in the mountains. The last thing I could see on the tape was the face of the SecForce squad leader, coming toward the camera and reaching out to grab it. His expression was a mix of shame and fear – not a look you often see on SecForce people.

They would have left the bodies there to be discovered, as a warning to anyone else thinking about subversion. However, we found out that not all the rich folks were against Jesús. Someone with a lot of money and a lot of clout learned about what had happened, presumably from Jesús' women friends, and got permission to take Jesús' body, bypass the morgue, and have it immured in the mausoleum space he'd reserved for himself – all in a few hours. If you've got enough money….

Months later, at a cocktail party, I heard the General telling someone that he never did give the order for Jesús' execution – that Jesús was released from his headquarters into the custody of local police and then lynched. But I had seen that videotape. And I knew that nothing moved around our headquarters without his permission.

The General's clever politics didn't do him much good, in the long run. He got transferred back to Washington and stuck in a minor office. Bishop Califas, on the other hand, went on to a lengthy career, mostly distinguished by his attacks on the followers of Jesús. The city of Los Angeles, of course, has gone from one crisis to another, and will probably end up in ruins, as Jesús is supposed to have predicted.

I retired before that could happen, glad to get out of it. I'm dying now, or so the doctors tell me. Otherwise I wouldn't be writing any of this down. What keeps coming back to my mind these days is the last image of Jesús on that videotape, as he looked at the SecForce man who was about to kill him. I thought I could read his lips and guess what he was saying. I hope he meant it for me, too. It was, "Father, forgive them. They don't know what they are doing."

[When you think about the real events of Jesus' Passion and death, how do you feel? What do you want to say to him?]

BACK TO THE BEGINNING
Luke 24a
[journal entry]

I sat quietly while my friend paged through my notebook. When she had finished we were silent together for a moment longer. Finally I asked, "What do you think of it?"

"It's interesting," she said.

"Thanks a lot."

"To be honest, I've heard some of these stories before, some of them in several different versions, and your take on some of them seems, well, a little strange."

"Now you think I'm making things up…?"

"No, it's just a bit different, that's all. Anyway, you can't end it that way. That's not the end of the story."

"I know, but I haven't got any idea how to tell the rest of it. It seems like it was…beyond words."

She looked thoughtful. "Maybe I've got something more for you."

"What would I do without you?" I wondered.

"Probably never finish your book, for one thing." She began rummaging among some old cartons in a corner of the garage. "My parents had a story from that time and I asked my father to write it down and he did, toward the end of his life. Here's what he wrote. His style is almost as weird as yours."

ON THE ROAD: THE DISCIPLES' STORY
Luke 24:1-35
[insert into notebook]

Luke 24:1-35
**Early in the morning the women went to the tomb...
When they went in, they did not find the body of the Lord Jesus...
Two men appeared to them, in shining clothes...
"He is not here; he is risen..."
They went back and told all this to the eleven and the rest...
Peter rushed to the tomb and saw what was there and came back wondering...**

That same day, two of them were going to a town called Emmaus.

All we wanted was to get out of town. It wasn't easy.

First, Mary M. wanted to borrow our car. It wasn't much, but it had wheels and a motor. My always generous spouse said all right. Mary M. had gone to the mausoleum with the rich guy who had claimed Jesús' body, and she wanted to go back and visit the place. So she and a couple of her friends took the car overnight and drove over to the west side and parked in front of the mausoleum until it opened in the morning.

According to what they said, there was no attendant to open it, it just opened. They went in and found the place where Jesús' body was supposed to be, but there was nothing there – just an empty place in the wall. Then, so she said, two people all dressed in white came along, and told them Jesús was alive. So they drove back over to the house we where we were staying and told us this story.

Then Simon wanted to borrow the car and go see for himself. He came back shaking his head. The scene at the mausoleum was as described, but he didn't know what to make of it.

Finally we got to reclaim our car and head for home. My cautious wife didn't want to get on the freeway. Who knew if the patrol was looking for people from our group? So we drove along surface streets. Ventura Boulevard was certainly slower than the freeway, but I couldn't see that it was any safer. But my wife had the wheel, and I was too depressed to argue with her.

We listened to the radio for a while. There was a talk show on, called "Religion in the Air," and to our surprise, they were able to talk about Jesús. The talk show host had several guests in his studio and was taking calls from listeners, too.

"I heard Jesús speak," said one caller, who did not want to identify herself, "and I thought he had some wise things to say. I think he may go down in history as an important moral teacher."

Another caller, likewise anonymous, intervened. "There was more to him than that. He was on the cutting edge of modern, progressive thought. If he's remembered in future generations, it will be as an inspiration to enlightened thinkers of every time."

"What do you think of that?" the host asked one of his studio guests.

"I wouldn't exaggerate his philosophical significance, though I can't deny his popular appeal. He captured well the disillusionment of our times. Is cynicism too strong a word? At any rate, he poked holes in the pretentiousness of certain people, and made sly cracks about our social institutions. I see him as a sort of a Garrison Kiellor with an edge to his wit, or a Jacques Derrida with a California accent."

"Let's hear from our next caller."

"You all don't get it. The man was a nut. He thought the world was going to end. He thought he was the beginning of a new human race. He deliberately got himself killed to bring things to a head. If he inspires some people to do good things, fine, but let's not take what he said too seriously."

"Well," said the host, "we certainly have a variety of opinions. Could it be that Jesús is like one of those inkblots, in which everyone sees what they're disposed to see? Let's hear from the professor of religious studies who's with us if he thinks we can come to any agreement."

"Certainly," said the professor. "I am in the process of convening a seminar, a meeting of experts in religion, to discuss the real Jesús. I've developed a system of voting by which we can decide what he really said and what people have put in his mouth. I'm sure that within a short time we can get a consensus on the historical Jesús."

"Will you include some of Jesús' most devoted followers in this seminar?"

"No, no religious fanatics. This will be an objective, scientific study."

Another caller broke through. "None of you (bleep) get it," he snarled. "Jesús was one of us. If he'd lived, we'd have had a leader for the revolution. We'll have our revolution anyway. We'll drive Pilato and his men out of California! We'll tear this (bleep) city down if we have to! We'll--"

"Time for a short break," said the host. "Now this."

"Well, that'll be the end of that show," said my prescient spouse, and turned the radio off. "For sure, none of them gets it. If people had just listened to Jesús, we'd have had a return to basic values: what we grew up with. Strong families. Communities where people shared with each other. In our little town, we could have appreciated those things. It was a mistake to go to the big city."

As they went along, talking about what had happened, and trying to figure it out...

83

> ...Jesus came up and went along with them. But they were prevented from recognizing him. He asked, "What have you been discussing?" "Are you the only resident of Jerusalem who does not know...?" "About what?" "About Jesus of Nazareth, and what happened to him... We hoped he was the one coming to save Israel. ...Some women of our group went to his tomb and found it empty, and claimed they had a vision of angels who said he is alive. But they did not see him." "Senseless and hardhearted people, you don't believe what the prophets said! It was necessary for the Savior to suffer." And he began to explain...

"Wait a minute," I objected. "You don't get it, either. Jesús' vision was bigger than just reestablishing traditional small town values. He wanted to save our people – make us realize that we're brothers and sisters."

"Charity begins at home," responded my resilient partner. "Speaking of which--" She hit the brakes, slamming me against the seat belt. "If we're going to talk about love of others, we ought to be willing to give that hitch-hiker a ride."

I hadn't even seen him. When we stopped, he came running up from behind and jumped in the back seat of the car. I couldn't get a good look at him: he was right behind me, and had a hat on, pulled down over his forehead. It made me nervous to pick up someone like that at such a time.

As we pulled back into traffic, the hitchhiker asked, "What have you two been talking about?" Like it was any of his business.

"Oh, just the news," I said.

"What's the news?" he asked.

My wife hit the brakes again, straining my neck muscles and the patience of the driver behind us. "Don't you read the papers? Or watch TV? You must be the only one in town who doesn't know what's going on. They arrested Jesús. And they killed him. And," my sometimes reckless spouse went on, "some of our group think he's coming back."

"All right," I said, "you've got us now. We're followers of Jesús. Turn us in if you want. What's ten or twenty years in prison? What do you get for being a follower of Jesús nowadays?"

"Life," said the hitchhiker.

"Since we've gone this far," I continued, "I might as well tell you, we had great hopes for Jesús' movement. We expected -- well, some of us did – that he was going to remake *la raza*, create a new nation -- but that's all over now."

"You don't get it, do you?" the hitchhiker said. "Don't you read the Scriptures? Don't you realize that everything that has happened is part of God's plan?" And he started talking to us about the Scriptures, quoting a lot from memory, but mostly explaining how it all fit together. He talked for a long time. It was fascinating.

When we got near Thousand Oaks, my ever practical wife said, "there's a good coffee shop here. It's getting late. Let's stop and get something to eat."

"Fine," said the hitchhiker. "You can let me off at any big intersection."

My decisive spouse wouldn't hear of it. She drove right to the door of the coffee shop and marched in, confident that we would follow her. I did so. This was certainly a cut above your standard coffee shop: there were white tablecloths, and a bottle of wine on the table, and the waiter brought a loaf of good bread without being asked.

The hitchhiker was slow about joining us. By the time he came in the door, we were seated, and the waiter had brought us the bread, and water, and menus.

The hitchhiker took off his hat and we had our first good look at him. We couldn't believe our eyes. He picked up the loaf of bread and broke it in half and gave us each a piece. "It's me," he said. "This is really me."

We stared at each other with our mouths open for a long minute. When we turned back toward our guest, he was gone. Somehow I knew it would do no good to run outside looking for him.

"I knew something was going on," said the love of my life. "While he was talking to us in the car, I thought my heart would explode."

Of course we had to go back to L.A. and tell the others. This time it was on the freeway, with me driving.

"No wonder nobody was getting it," I said. "No one could get it, unless he came and showed himself to them. No one could believe that the Kingdom of God is still coming, until he explained it, like he did to us."

"It's not just a matter of explaining, either," pointed out my perceptive partner. "You have to get some of the spirit of it – and he has to give that to you, I guess – the spirit that was in him."

"*Is* in him," I corrected her.

We made it back to the house in L.A. and told everyone there what had happened. Of course Simon had to top our story – he had seen Jesús first, and convinced the rest that Jesús was alive.

As they approached their destination, he acted as if he were going on. They insisted: "Stay with us!" … While they were at table, he took bread, and blessed and broke it and gave it to them. And their eyes were opened, and they recognized him; but he disappeared. They said, "Weren't our hearts burning within us, as he spoke to us on the road and explained the Scriptures to us?"

They went back to Jerusalem and found the eleven and the others, who told them, "The Lord truly has risen, and has appeared to Simon!"

While they were talking, Jesus was there in the midst of them… He shared food with them… He said, "These things I told you while I was still with you; this is what was foretold by the prophets… You are the witnesses. I am sending to you what my Father promised – power from on high. Wait for it, here in the City."…
…He left them and was taken up to heaven.

Acts 1:4-9

He told them to wait in Jerusalem. "You will be baptized with the Holy Spirit soon."
"Lord, is this the time when you will restore the Kingdom to Israel?"
"All you need to know is that you will receive the Holy Spirit, and will be my witnesses – to the ends of the earth."

It didn't matter. What mattered was that he was alive. And more than alive. In the days that followed, he'd drop in, unannounced, usually when we were sharing a meal, and have a bite with us. He'd talk with us about why things happened the way they did, how everything in past history led up to these days, and these days were just a preparation for what was going to come. Every time he talked to us, we were on fire. It was not just that he was alive, but that he seemed to be the only one in the whole world who was really alive, and was waiting for the rest of us to catch up with him.

We had just a dim idea of what was coming. Was he going to make himself known to others the way he had come to us? Was he going to give some of his own spirit to everyone? Would that mean the coming of God's reign?

We didn't know exactly. We could only wait and pray.

[In what ways is the risen Lord Jesus Christ present to you?
In what ways is he still to come?}

ON THE ROAD, STILL
Luke 24:36-53
[journal entry]

Acts 2:42

They carried on the teaching of the Apostles, and the community life, and the breaking of bread and prayer.

I finished reading what her father had written and sat in silence for a few moments.

"What about you?" I asked.

"What about me?"

"Did Jesús ever speak to you?"

"Not like my parents. But I figure he's made himself known to me through them. And through the rest of our brothers and sisters, when we read the Book together and talk about it and break bread together. He's there."

"And has he inspired you to…?"

"To put my faith in him, to speak about him, to sing about freedom – yes. To feel like I've arrived, like I've got nothing more to learn? No, I'm still a pilgrim, like everyone else. And what about you?"

"I accept what you've told me," I said, realizing that that didn't answer her question. "But I'm still not sure what to do with all you've given me."

"I thought you were going to write a book," she said.

"I was. I mean, I am. But I don't know how to put it together so it will say what I want to say. I'm not sure I even have the nerve to put it out there for the public…and what public, anyway?"

"Sometimes you just have to do what's right and let God take care of the results. Isn't that in your notebook somewhere?"

"I guess I need some of your spirit."

"Jesús' spirit. Well, it'll come to you. You know what you have to do. Just wait."

"You sound very confident."

Acts 1:14

They
persevered
in prayer...

Acts 2:4

...and they
were filled
with the
Holy Spirit.

"I am. I'm going to pray for you to receive God's spirit. And you'll pray for that, too, won't you? And you know what Jesús said about that kind of prayer."

It was getting late. I looked at my watch. "It's time for me to hit the road," I said. I thanked her, very sincerely, for what she had shown me, and went out into the evening and drove away.

I had a way to go yet before I got where I was going. Be patient and pray, I thought. Her parents had done that. Simon and the others had done that. And look what they had accomplished, in time. But that's another story. Maybe another book.

[What unfinished business is there in your own life?]

The real Luke, of course, did write that second volume, the Acts of the Apostles. My imaginary "Luke" hasn't even got the first book finished. But he's on the way.

Made in the USA
Lexington, KY
26 February 2010